SEDGEWOOD™
BOOK OF BAKING

SEDGEWOOD™
BOOK OF BAKING

Sedgewood™ Press

Published by Sedgewood™ Press

For Sedgewood™ Press
Editorial Director: Jane Ross
Managing Editor: Gale Kremer
Production Manager: Bill Rose

Produced for Sedgewood™ Press by
Marshall Cavendish House
58 Old Compton Street
LONDON W1V 5PA

For Marshall Cavendish
Consultant Editor: Virginia Colton
Editor-in-Chief: Barbara Bloch
Senior Editor: Rita Barrett
Special Recipe Development:
Rita Barrett
Designer: Brenda Morrison
Production Editor: Maggi McCormick

First printing 1983
© Marshall Cavendish Limited 1983

Library of Congress
Catalog Card Number: 82-51036

Distributed in the Trade by
Van Nostrand Reinhold Company

ISBN 0-442-28102-1

Printed in the United States of America

Cherry-Topped Cheesecake (page 62)

CONTENTS

Rum Savarin (page 158)

Picture Credits:

Bryce Attwell: 131
Paul Bussell: 47, 53, 89, 136
Patrick Cocklin: 117
Alan Duns: Front cover, back cover, 2, 8,
    10(T), 17, 51, 69, 91, 127, 132(BR), 137,
    143, 145, 146(BL), 146(BR), 157, 161, 163,
    167, 169
John Elliot: 15, 81
Edmund Goldspink: 83
Melvin Grey: 173, 179
John Hall: 75
Gina Harris: 98
James Jackson: 67, 78(BL), 79, 93, 121
Michael Kay: 10(BR), 27
Paul Kemp: 35(T), 49, 57, 132(BL), 139, 153,
    171
John Kevern: 31
Chris Knaggs: 1, 4, 6, 23, 29, 39, 55, 63,
    107(B), 116, 119, 129, 151, 159
Don Last: 9, 181

David Levin: 33, 35(B), 43, 45, 73(R),
    107(T), 126, 155(T), 155(B), 171(T)
Fred Mancini: 185
Peter Myers: 58(BR), 77, 78(BR), 101,
    108(BL), 111, 113, 115, 140, 177, 183
Roger Phillips: 13, 37, 58(T), 58(BL), 85,
    105, 108(T), 108(BR), 123, 134, 146(T),
    149, 187
Iain Reid: 65, 71, 78(T), 87, 132(T), 135, 141
Mike Vines/Cadbury Typhoo: 21
Paul Webster: 165
Paul Williams: 10(BL), 19, 25, 41, 73(L), 95,
    103, 125

6

INTRODUCTION

This is a book dedicated to the thousands of people who love to bake, but aren't always satisfied with how well their baking comes out, or with what they can bake to their own satisfaction. If you enjoy baking, that's half the battle. Enthusiasm is certainly the prime ingredient in baking success. By itself, however, it won't get you very far. Reliable recipes, too, are important but they only contribute to success, they don't guarantee it. If you're dissatisfied with your baking, what you need is the help this book gives.

The help takes several different forms, but the major assistance comes right at the start of each chapter. Any section you turn to — Cakes, Cheesecakes and Meringues, Pies and Pastry, Cookies, Quick Breads and Muffins, Yeast Breads — opens with a page of pointers that relate directly to that kind of baking. Before you even begin to browse through the recipes, let alone pick out ones you'd like to try, the section opener fortifies you with the clues to success.

Each section, too, covers a wide spectrum, from very simple though somewhat unusual to quite intricate gourmet specialties. There are plenty of recipes for those — you may be one of them — who are perfectly happy to stay with the simpler kinds of baking. We're all for that, if that's what you prefer. We've even included a chapter on varying mixes and being clever with such conveniences as frozen bread dough. What we want is what you want: consistently delicious results with whatever you choose to bake.

We hope, though, that this volume will tempt you to venture beyond simplicity to some techniques you've never tried — perhaps one of the incomparable yeast breads, which many cooks are timid about tackling. What has seemed intimidating from a distance will turn out not to be forbidding at all, once the method has been clearly explained. You might start with all-American white bread, and go on to rye, whole-wheat or French. When you know exactly what you are doing, you can move confidently in any direction.

Then there is a third area, and a most rewarding one to delve into: the more elaborate baked specialties, often European, that call for special skills. (They frequently require special equipment as well — see the recommendations that follow.) Sometimes it's

BASIC NECESSITIES

General
Citrus zester or grater
Electric mixer
Large wooden cutting
 board
Liquid and dry measuring
 cups
Measuring spoons
Mixing bowls
Oven thermometer
Rubber spatula
Sharp knives
Sifter
Wide metal spatula
Wire racks
Wire whisk
Wooden spoons

Cakes
8- or 9-inch round cake
 pans
9- and 10-inch springform
 pans
10-inch tube pan
9-inch square pan
7 × 11-inch oblong pan
9 × 13-inch oblong pan

Pies
9- or 10-inch pie plates
Aluminum foil
Pastry blender
Rolling pin

Cookies
Cookie sheets

Yeast Breads and Quick Breads
Biscuit cutters
Loaf pans
Muffin pans
Yeast thermometer

Clockwise: Corn Bread, Corn Sticks, Corn Muffins (page 142)

a matter of manipulation, of handling an unfamiliar shape or kind of dough. Cake rolls are one example; choux paste, which becomes cream puffs and eclairs, is another. Croissants and brioches also come to mind. The elegant gateaus (French for "fancy cakes") are notable for their embellishment: decorative frostings, chocolate curls, edging with chopped nuts. Where these are called for, the recipe pages are ready with tips to guide you in preparing them—and getting them, picture-pretty, onto your cake.

That brings up another form of instruction you will find throughout the book: full-color photographs of every recipe, partly (we must admit) to intrigue you, but mainly to show you how the finished product should look. And will look, if you follow carefully our good advice.

Advance pointers, technique tips, full-color photos. Fine as far as they go, but they leave one significant question still unanswered: Isn't it expensive to equip a kitchen for so many kinds of baking? It can be very costly if you buy everything at once, or the wrong things, or equipment you find you really don't use. It is best to develop some dexterity with basic tools and utensils and some sense of where your baking interests lie first. Then you can add new equipment, and master its use, gradually, as you need or want to. The equipment inventory (right and left) divides baking equipment into two groups: basic necessities and supplements for special purposes. It should help you to judge the efficiency of your present kitchen, and to select additions to it that will be worthwhile.

SUPPLEMENTS FOR SPECIAL PURPOSES

Blender and/or food
  processor
Brioche mold
Bundt pan
Cookie cutters
Cookie press
Corn stick pan
Croissant cutter
Double boiler
Fancy cake molds
French bread pan
Jelly-roll pan
Miniature tart pans
Parchment paper
Pastry bag and assorted
  tips
Pastry blender
Pastry wheel
Pie weights
Small icing spatula
10-inch quiche/flan pan

Cherry Cloverleaf Buns (page 180)

CAKES

More often than not, a homemade cake is either a gift of love to someone or the special ending of a party meal. And since most cakes can be made ahead of the time they are to be served, it should be possible to set aside enough time for unhurried baking.

Most cake recipes are exact chemical formulas and, when you follow directions carefully, should turn out exactly as expected. The hints and tips that follow provide the know-how you need for a perfect cake every time.

HINTS AND TIPS

● Assemble all the ingredients before you start baking. Allow enough time for refrigerated food such as butter, margarine, eggs or milk to soften or come to room temperature.

● Separate eggs, if necessary, while they are still cold. Then allow them to come to room temperature.

● Use the pan size called for in the recipe and prepare the pan before you mix the cake batter.

● Measure all your ingredients very carefully. Be sure to use both liquid and dry measuring cups as appropriate. Level dry ingredients with the back of a knife.

● Preheat the oven 10 to 15 minutes before you plan to use it. Use an oven thermometer to be sure you are baking at the correct temperature.

● Follow the recipe instructions carefully with regard to the order in which ingredients are combined and the amount of time necessary for mixing. Overmixing will make the batter heavy and result in a heavy cake.

● Never fill cake pans more than two-thirds full.

● When you pour the batter into the prepared pans, make sure it is distributed evenly. Tap the filled cake pans gently on a flat surface to eliminate air bubbles.

● Place the cake pans in the center of the oven. If you are baking more than one pan at a time, be sure the pans don't touch each other or the walls of the oven. Air must be able to circulate freely around pans.

● Use a timer and check the cake after the minimum baking time. Bake longer if necessary, but check every few minutes.

● A cake is done when a cake tester or toothpick inserted in the center comes out clean, or the surface of the cake springs back when lightly pressed. Use a tester if a toothpick won't go deep enough.

● Follow the recipe directions for cooling. Most cakes are cooled in the pan on a wire rack until the cake pulls away from the sides of the pan. The cake is then removed from the pan and cooling is finished on the rack. Angel food and chiffon cakes are cooled completely in an inverted pan before they are removed.

● Cool cakes completely before filling and frosting.

Clockwise: Strawberry Cream Cake
(page 50), French Walnut Roll (page 26),
Pound Cake Ring (page 12)

POUND CAKE RING

SERVES 10 TO 12

2 ¼ cups cake flour
1 teaspoon baking powder
½ teaspoon salt
1 cup butter or margarine, softened
1 ½ cups granulated sugar
4 eggs
2 teaspoons vanilla
grated peel of 1 orange
1 cup dairy sour cream
confectioners sugar

1. Preheat oven to 325°F. Grease 10-inch springform pan with fluted bottom or 12-cup Bundt pan.

2. Sift flour, baking powder and salt together; set aside.

3. Place butter in large mixing bowl and beat until creamy. Gradually add sugar, beating at medium speed until light and fluffy. Add eggs, 1 at a time, beating well after each addition. Beat in vanilla and orange peel. Gradually add flour mixture to creamed mixture alternately with sour cream, beating at medium speed until well combined.

4. Spread batter evenly in prepared pan; tap pan gently on countertop to remove any air bubbles. Smooth top and bake 1 hour to 1 hour 5 minutes, or until cake tester inserted 1 inch from center comes out clean.

5. Cool in pan on wire rack 10 minutes. Invert from pan onto wire rack, carefully remove pan, and cool completely on rack. Dust top of cake with sifted confectioners sugar just before serving.

Picture, see page 10

HINTS AND TIPS

The secret to proper creaming of butter and sugar is in the beating process. Butter must be softened to be beaten until creamy. It will take at least 6 to 7 minutes of constant beating at medium speed to cream the butter and the sugar together thoroughly. The mixture is properly creamed when it has become light and very fluffy.

PINEAPPLE UPSIDE-DOWN CAKE

SERVES 9

TOPPING

¼ cup butter or margarine
½ cup firmly packed light brown sugar
1 can (20 ounces) sliced pineapple, well drained
5 maraschino or candied cherries, halved

CAKE

1½ cups cake flour
⅔ cup granulated sugar
2 teaspoons baking powder
½ teaspoon salt
⅔ cup milk
5 tablespoons butter, margarine or shortening
1 egg
1 teaspoon vanilla

1. Topping: Preheat oven to 350°F. Place ¼ cup butter in 9-inch square baking pan and place pan in oven until melted. Remove pan from oven and stir in brown sugar, spreading it evenly in pan. Arrange pineapple slices over brown sugar mixture and place a halved cherry, rounded side down, in center of each pineapple slice; set aside.

2. Cake: Place all ingredients in large mixing bowl and beat at low speed about 1 minute, or until blended. Increase speed to medium and beat 2 minutes, scraping sides of bowl occasionally.

3. Pour batter into pan, spreading it to edges, being careful not to disturb pineapple slices. Bake 40 to 45 minutes, or until cake is lightly browned and pulls away from sides of pan.

4. Cool in pan on wire rack 2 minutes. Place serving plate over cake and carefully invert pan and plate together. Keep pan over cake about 2 minutes and then carefully remove pan. Serve warm or chilled.

GOLDEN CITRUS CAKE

SERVES 10 TO 12

CAKE
2½ cups all-purpose flour
2 teaspoons baking powder
½ teaspoon salt
¾ cup butter or margarine,
    softened
1½ cups sugar
4 eggs, separated
2 tablespoons lemon juice
1 teaspoon grated lemon peel
2 teaspoons grated orange peel
¾ cup orange juice

CITRUS GLAZE
3 tablespoons butter or margarine
2 cups confectioners sugar, sifted
3 to 4 tablespoons orange juice
1 tablespoon grated orange peel

1. Cake: Preheat oven to 350°F. Grease and flour 10-inch cake mold or tube pan.

2. Sift flour, baking powder and salt together; set aside. Cream butter until very smooth. Add sugar and beat until light and fluffy. Add egg yolks, 1 at a time, beating well after each addition. Beat in lemon juice and lemon and orange peels until well blended. Add flour mixture alternately with orange juice, beating at low speed just until blended.

3. Beat egg whites until stiff peaks form. Fold beaten whites into batter until no white streaks remain.

4. Pour batter into prepared pan and smooth top. Bake 50 to 60 minutes, or until cake tester inserted in center comes out clean. Cool in pan on wire rack 15 minutes. Invert from pan onto rack and cool completely.

5. Citrus Glaze: Melt butter in small saucepan. Remove from heat and let cool slightly. Gradually stir in confectioners sugar. Add orange juice, 1 tablespoon at a time, stirring until mixture is smooth and glaze is good pouring consistency. Stir in orange peel.

6. Place cake on serving plate and spoon half the glaze over cake. Let stand 10 minutes. Spoon remaining glaze over cake, covering it completely. Let stand until glaze is set.

COCOA-CHOCOLATE LAYER CAKE

SERVES 8 TO 10

CAKE
1¾ cups all-purpose flour
½ cup unsweetened cocoa
1½ teaspoons baking soda
1 teaspoon salt
¾ cup butter or margarine, softened
1½ cups sugar
1 teaspoon vanilla
3 eggs
1 cup milk

WHIPPED CREAM FROSTING
2 cups heavy cream
½ cup sifted confectioners sugar
1½ teaspoons vanilla
2 ounces semisweet or milk chocolate

1. Cake: Preheat oven to 350°F. Grease and flour two 8-inch round cake pans.

2. Sift flour, cocoa, baking soda and salt together; set aside. Cream butter until light in large mixing bowl. Add sugar and beat until light and fluffy. Beat in vanilla. Add eggs, 1 at a time, beating well after each addition. Add flour mixture alternately with milk, beating well after each addition and ending with flour mixture. Divide batter equally between prepared pans and smooth tops.

3. Bake 25 to 30 minutes, or until tops spring back when lightly pressed. Cool in pans on wire racks 10 minutes. Invert from pans onto racks and cool completely.

4. Whipped Cream Frosting: Beat cream until thick. Gradually beat in confectioners sugar and vanilla; continue beating until firm and thick enough to spread. Spoon about 1 cup of whipped cream into pastry bag fitted with medium-size star tip; set aside in refrigerator.

5. To assemble and decorate cake, place 1 layer, bottom side up, on serving plate; spread with about one-third of remaining whipped cream. Top with second layer. Spread remaining whipped cream over sides and top of cake, smoothing with flat-bladed knife or icing spatula.

6. Remove pastry bag from refrigerator and pipe swirls or rosettes around top and bottom edges of cake. Grate chocolate over top or make chocolate curls and use to decorate cake.

HINTS AND TIPS

To make chocolate curls, hold the chocolate, in its wrapper, in the palm of your hand for about 2 to 3 minutes, or just long enough to soften the outside of the chocolate bar. Remove the wrapper and shave the chocolate into curls with a vegetable peeler. Let the chocolate curls fall on a waxed paper-lined flat dish. Refrigerate about 10 to 15 minutes to harden. Remove from the refrigerator and carefully slip a toothpick through the hole in the curls to lift. Arrange decoratively on top of cake.

To grate chocolate, hold a bar of chocolate firmly against the coarse side of a cheese grater and grate onto waxed paper in quick up and down strokes. Use grated chocolate to decorate cakes, mousses, souffles, pies or other desserts.

LIGHT FRUIT CAKE

SERVES 12 TO 16

CAKE
¾ cup chopped candied pineapple
¾ cup chopped candied cherries
½ cup chopped mixed candied fruit
⅓ cup chopped candied citron
¼ cup chopped crystallized ginger
1 cup chopped almonds, pecans or walnuts
2½ cups all-purpose flour
1 teaspoon baking powder
1 cup butter or margarine
1½ cups sugar
4 eggs
½ cup orange juice

DECORATIVE TOPPING
3 tablespoons apple jelly
shelled whole Brazil nuts
candied pineapple
candied cherries
whole blanched almonds
walnut halves

1. **Cake:** Preheat oven to 325°F. Grease deep 8-inch round cake pan or springform pan. Line bottom and sides with double thickness of waxed paper or aluminum foil, extending the paper 2 to 3 inches above rim of pan. Grease the paper.

2. Place candied pineapple, cherries, mixed fruit, citron, ginger and nuts in a bowl. Sprinkle with ½ cup flour and toss until well coated; set aside.

3. Sift remaining 2 cups flour and baking powder together; set aside.

4. Cream butter in a large mixing bowl until light. Add sugar and beat until light and fluffy. Add eggs, 1 at a time, beating well after each addition.

5. Add flour mixture alternately with orange juice, beating until well blended. Beat 2 minutes at medium speed, scraping sides of bowl occasionally.

6. Add fruit-nut mixture and stir with wooden spoon until well blended. Spoon mixture into prepared pan and smooth top.

7. Bake 2 hours 15 minutes, or until cake tester inserted in center comes out clean. Cool completely in pan on wire rack. Remove from pan and peel off paper.

8. **Decorative topping:** Heat apply jelly in small saucepan until melted; let cool. Brush top of cake with melted jelly. Arrange row of Brazil nuts around outside edge of cake. Arrange a row of candied pineapple pieces inside nuts, and then a row of candied cherries. Arrange almonds and walnut halves in center of cake. Brush top of decorated cake with remaining melted jelly. Store in cool, dark place or refrigerator 1 to 2 days before serving.

HINTS AND TIPS

Fruit cakes, filled with dried and candied fruit and lots of spices, keep well and should be made in advance because their flavor improves if they are allowed to mellow. Since it is traditional to serve this kind of cake at holiday time, plan to make it in advance of the holidays. Fruit cake can be wrapped and stored in a covered metal cake tin, placed in the refrigerator, and kept for several months. This will allow the fruit cake to "ripen" and will enhance its flavor.

Tossing the fruit and nuts with flour before adding them to the batter prevents them from sinking to the bottom of the cake.

DEVIL'S FOOD CAKE

SERVES 8 TO 10

CAKE
2½ cups sifted cake flour
1½ teaspoons baking soda
½ teaspoon baking powder
½ teaspoon salt
½ cup butter or margarine, softened
1 cup granulated sugar
¾ cup firmly packed light brown sugar
3 eggs
1 teaspoon vanilla
4 squares (4 ounces) unsweetened chocolate, melted
1½ cups buttermilk

VANILLA BUTTERCREAM FILLING
4 tablespoons butter or margarine, softened
1½ cups sifted confectioners sugar
1 to 1½ tablespoons milk or light cream

CHOCOLATE BUTTERCREAM FROSTING:
1 package (6 ounces) semisweet chocolate morsels
6 tablespoons butter or margarine, softened
4 cups confectioners sugar
2 egg yolks
about 2 tablespoons milk or light cream

1. Cake: Preheat oven to 350°F. Grease and flour two 9-inch round cake pans.

2. Sift flour, baking soda, baking powder and salt together; set aside. Cream butter, granulated sugar and brown sugar together in large mixing bowl until light and fluffy. Beat in eggs and vanilla until well blended. Beat in melted chocolate.

3. Add flour mixture alternately with buttermilk to chocolate mixture, beating well after each addition. Divide batter equally between prepared pans and smooth tops.

4. Bake 30 to 35 minutes, or until toothpick inserted in center of each cake comes out clean. Cool in pans on wire racks 10 minutes. Invert from pans onto racks and cool completely.

5. Vanilla Buttercream Filling: Cream butter until light. Beat in confectioners sugar. Gradually beat in milk, 1 teaspoon at a time, until filling is good spreading consistency.

6. Chocolate Buttercream Frosting: Melt chocolate in top of double boiler; let cool. Beat butter in mixing bowl until light and fluffy. Beat in confectioners sugar. Add melted chocolate and egg yolks; beat until well blended. Gradually beat in milk until frosting is good spreading consistency.

7. To fill and frost cake, place 1 layer, bottom side up, on serving plate; spread with Vanilla Buttercream Filling. Top with second layer. Spread Chocolate Buttercream Frosting over sides and top of cake, swirling decoratively with flat-bladed knife or icing spatula.

HINTS AND TIPS

If you don't keep buttermilk on hand, substitute sour milk. To make sour milk, stir 1 tablespoon lemon juice or white vinegar into 1 cup whole milk and let stand 5 minutes before using. Cultured buttermilk is now available in powdered form in canisters and 3-ounce packages. Simply store it in the pantry and reconstitute with water when you have a recipe that calls for buttermilk.

GINGER-APPLE CAKE

TOPPING
¼ cup butter or margarine
½ cup firmly packed light brown
  sugar
1 to 2 medium-size tart apples

CAKE
1½ cups cake flour
1½ teaspoons baking powder
½ teaspoon salt
1½ teaspoons ground ginger
½ teaspoon grated nutmeg
⅓ cup butter or margarine
1 cup firmly packed light brown
  sugar
2 eggs
grated peel and juice of 1 lemon
½ cup milk

1. **Topping:** Preheat oven to 350°F. Place butter in 9-inch round cake pan and place in oven until butter is melted. Remove from the oven and stir in brown sugar, spreading it evenly in pan.

2. Peel, core and slice apples. Arrange apple slices over brown sugar mixture in circular pattern, covering bottom of pan completely; set aside.

3. **Cake:** Sift flour, baking powder, salt, ginger and nutmeg together; set aside.

4. Cream butter in mixing bowl until light. Beat in brown sugar until light and fluffy. Add eggs, 1 at a time, beating well after each addition. Add lemon peel and juice and beat until well blended. Add flour-spice mixture and milk alternately, beating thoroughly after each addition until well combined.

5. Carefully pour batter into prepared pan, spreading it evenly over apple slices. Bake 40 to 45 minutes, or until toothpick inserted in center comes out clean. Remove from oven and let stand in pan on wire rack 2 minutes. Place warm serving plate over cake and carefully invert pan and plate together. Let stand with pan over cake 3 minutes. Gently remove pan. Let cool completely on plate or serve warm. Spoon whipped cream over top or pass separately at table, if desired.

VARIATIONS
Peach-Ginger Cake: Add ½ teaspoon cinnamon to melted butter-brown sugar mixture in pan. Omit apples and use 3 or 4 firm fresh peaches, peeled, pitted and sliced. Omit lemon peel and juice in batter and substitute 1 tablespoon grated orange peel. If fresh peaches are not available, use 1 can (16 ounces) sliced peaches, drained.
Pear-Ginger Cake: Add ¼ cup chopped walnuts or pecans to melted butter-brown sugar mixture in pan. Omit apples and use 1 can (16 ounces) sliced pears, drained.

CREAM-FILLED CRUMB CAKE

SERVES 8 TO 10

CREAM FILLING
1½ tablespoons cornstarch
⅓ cup sugar
¼ teaspoon salt
1½ cups milk or light cream
3 egg yolks, beaten
1 tablespoon butter or margarine
1½ teaspoons vanilla or 1 teaspoon
  vanilla and ½ teaspoon almond
  extract
1 to 2 tablespoons kirsch (optional)

CRUMB TOPPING
¼ cup all-purpose flour
¼ cup granulated sugar
½ teaspoon cinnamon
3 tablespoons butter or margarine
¼ cup chopped almonds
confectioners sugar

CAKE
1¼ cups sifted cake flour
1½ teaspoons baking powder
¼ teaspoon salt
3 eggs, separated
1 cup granulated sugar
1 tablespoon lemon juice
½ cup warm milk
sifted confectioners sugar

1. Cream Filling: Stir cornstarch, sugar and salt together in saucepan. Add milk and stir with wire whisk until mixture is smooth and no lumps remain. Place saucepan over low heat and cook, stirring constantly, until mixture comes to a boil. Boil 1 minute. Remove from heat and stir 4 tablespoons hot milk mixture into beaten egg yolks. Slowly pour egg yolk mixture back into saucepan, stirring constantly. Return to low heat and cook 1 to 2 minutes, stirring until thickened (do not let mixture boil). Remove from heat and stir in butter until melted. Let cool slightly and stir in vanilla and kirsch. Press a piece of waxed paper onto surface of filling and refrigerate until needed.

2. Crumb Topping: Combine flour, sugar and cinnamon in small bowl. Cut in butter until mixture is consistency of coarse crumbs. Stir in almonds until well blended; set aside.

3. Cake: Preheat oven to 350°F. Grease 9-inch springform pan. Line bottom of pan with waxed paper and grease the paper.

4. Sift flour, baking powder and salt together; set aside.

5. Beat egg yolks in mixing bowl until thick and lemon-colored. Add sugar and continue beating until fluffy. Beat in lemon juice and milk until blended. Gradually fold in flour mixture until thoroughly combined.

6. Beat egg whites until stiff peaks form. Fold into egg-flour mixture. Pour batter into prepared pan and smooth top.

7. Bake in center of oven 25 minutes. Remove from oven and sprinkle with Crumb Topping. Return to oven and bake 20 to 25 minutes, or until cake tester inserted in center comes out clean.

8. Cool in pan on wire rack 10 minutes. Carefully remove side of pan and cool completely on rack.

9. Slide wide spatula under cake and carefully lift onto serving plate. Cut cake in half horizontally with serrated knife to make 2 layers. Carefully lift off top crumb-covered layer; set aside. Spread bottom layer with chilled Cream Filling. Top with crumb-covered layer. Refrigerate until ready to serve. Sprinkle with sifted confectioners sugar just before serving. Cut with very sharp knife.

FRENCH WALNUT ROLL

SERVES 8

CAKE
2 tablespoons all-purpose flour
½ teaspoon baking powder
¼ teaspoon salt
6 eggs, separated
½ cup granulated sugar
1 cup coarsely ground walnuts
confectioners sugar

FILLING
2 cups heavy cream
½ cup granulated sugar
confectioners sugar
8 walnut halves

1. Cake: Preheat oven to 350°F. Grease 10 × 15-inch jelly-roll pan. Line pan with waxed paper and grease the paper.

2. Sift flour, baking powder and salt together; set aside.

3. Beat egg yolks and granulated sugar together in top of double boiler until thick and lemon-colored. Set over (not in) simmering water, and continue beating about 5 minutes, or until mixture falls in a thick ribbon when beaters are lifted. Remove from heat and continue beating until mixture is cool (mixture will be very thick). Fold in ground walnuts. Thoroughly wash beaters.

4. Beat egg whites until stiff peaks form. Stir large heaping spoonful of beaten whites into walnut mixture to lighten. Fold in remaining beaten whites. Sprinkle flour mixture on top of walnut mixture and thoroughly, but gently, fold in. Pour mixture into prepared pan, spreading to edges of pan and smoothing surface with small spatula. Bake 18 to 20 minutes, or until cake springs back when lightly pressed.

5. While cake is baking, place large clean dish towel on work surface. Sprinkle towel generously with confectioners sugar. When cake is done, invert cake immediately onto sugared towel. Remove pan and carefully peel off waxed paper. Trim off any stiff, crusty edges. While cake is still hot, carefully roll up, jelly-roll style, with towel, starting from narrow end. Place wrapped, rolled cake, seam-side down, on wire rack and cool completely.

6. Filling: Beat cream until soft peaks form. Add granulated sugar and continue beating until firm. Carefully unroll cake. Spread three-fourths of whipped cream over cake. Gently reroll cake without towel. Place cake on long, flat serving plate; dust with sifted confectioners sugar. Spoon remaining whipped cream into pastry bag fitted with star tip; pipe whipped cream decoratively down center of cake. Decorate with walnut halves.

> **HINTS AND TIPS**
> To prevent the cake from cracking, it must be rolled while very warm. A clean linen dish towel works best and prevents the cake from sticking together while it cools.

PETITS FOURS

MAKES ABOUT 4 DOZEN

CAKE
¾ cup cake flour
1 teaspoon baking powder
½ teaspoon salt
4 eggs, room temperature
¾ cup sugar
1 teaspoon vanilla or ½ teaspoon
    almond extract

APRICOT GLAZE
1½ cups apricot or raspberry jam
    or preserves

SUGAR GLAZE
4 cups confectioners sugar
2 tablespoons light corn syrup
1 teaspoon vanilla or ½ teaspoon
    almond extract
2 squares (2 ounces) semisweet
    chocolate, melted

DECORATION
crystallized candy flowers
chocolate leaves
silver dragées

HINTS AND TIPS
To make chocolate leaves, brush melted semisweet chocolate onto underside of clean, unblemished rose or small ivy leaves. Place coated leaves, chocolate side up, on waxed paper and let stand until chocolate is firm. Gently peel off leaves and place the ''chocolate leaves'' on waxed paper-lined plate until needed.

---

1. Cake: Preheat oven to 350°F. Grease 9 × 13-inch baking pan and line with waxed paper. Grease and flour the paper.

2. Sift flour, baking powder and salt together; set aside. Beat eggs in large mixing bowl at high speed until foamy. Gradually add sugar, beating at high speed about 8 minutes, or until mixture is thick and lemon-colored. Beat in vanilla. Gradually fold in flour mixture until blended.

3. Spread in prepared pan and smooth top. Bake 20 to 25 minutes, or until center of cake springs back when lightly pressed. Cool in pan on wire rack 10 minutes. Invert onto rack, remove pan, peel off waxed paper, and cool completely.

4. Apricot Glaze: Press jam through strainer into small saucepan. Place over low heat. Add ⅓ cup cold water and stir until mixture is blended and jam is melted. Remove from heat and cool slightly.

5. Place cake on work surface and trim off any crusty edges. Cut into 1½-inch squares, small rectangles, rounds or triangles. Spear cake pieces, one at a time, with a fork and dip sides and bottom into apricot glaze to coat. Place cake pieces, uncoated side down, on wire racks set over cookie sheets. Let stand about 45 minutes until glaze is set.

6. Sugar Glaze: Place confectioners sugar, corn syrup and 4 tablespoons water in top of double boiler; set over simmering water. Cook, stirring constantly, until sugar is dissolved and mixture is smooth. Remove from heat and stir in vanilla. Pour half of mixture into small bowl set over pan of hot water and stir in melted chocolate. Spoon Vanilla Glaze over half of cakes, covering them completely. Spoon Chocolate Glaze over remaining cakes. Scrape up glazes that have dripped onto cookie sheets and reheat to pouring consistency, adding 1 teaspoon hot water to thin, if necessary. Spoon over cakes for smooth, glossy finish. Let stand until glaze is set. Remove cakes from racks with long, thin spatula and place in paper candy liners, if desired. Decorate tops with crystallized candy flowers, chocolate leaves, silver dragées or other decorations.

MOCHA-SPICE CAKE

SERVES 6 TO 8

CAKE
2 cups cake flour
3 teaspoons baking powder
1 teaspoon salt
1 teaspoon cinnamon
½ teaspoon ground allspice
½ teaspoon ground cloves
½ teaspoon ground ginger
½ cup butter or margarine
¾ cup granulated sugar
½ cup firmly packed light brown
  sugar
1 teaspoon vanilla
¾ cup milk

CREAMY MOCHA FROSTING
1 cup sweet butter
1 tablespoon instant coffee powder
1 cup sugar
4 egg yolks
¾ cup toasted, chopped almonds

1. Cake: Preheat oven to 350°F. Grease two 8-inch round cake pans. Line bottoms of pans with waxed paper. Grease and flour the paper and sides of pans.

2. Sift flour, baking powder, salt, cinnamon, allspice, cloves and ginger together; set aside. Cream butter and sugars together until light and fluffy. Beat in vanilla until blended. Add flour mixture alternately with milk, beating at low speed, just until blended.

3. Divide batter equally between prepared pans and smooth tops. Bake 25 to 30 minutes, or until toothpick inserted in center of each cake comes out clean. Cool in pans on wire racks 10 minutes. Invert from pans onto racks, peel off waxed paper, and cool completely.

4. Creamy Mocha Frosting: Beat butter in mixing bowl until smooth and creamy. Dissolve coffee in 1 tablespoon hot water and beat into butter until well blended; set aside. Place sugar in heavy saucepan and pour in ¼ cup water; stir to dissolve. Place saucepan over medium heat and bring to a boil. Set a candy thermometer in sugar syrup and boil gently until temperature registers 230°F to 234°F (soft ball stage). Remove from heat. Beat egg yolks in mixing bowl at high speed until thick and lemon-colored. Add sugar syrup, in thin, steady stream, to beaten yolks, beating constantly. Continue beating until mixture is very thick and completely cooled. Gradually beat in butter-coffee mixture until well blended. Refrigerate a short time to give frosting good spreading consistency.

5. To assemble and decorate cake, place 1 layer, bottom side up, on clean work surface. Spread with one-third of Creamy Mocha Frosting; top with second layer. Spread one-third of remaining frosting around sides of cake. Spread ½ cup chopped almonds on a sheet of waxed paper. Hold cake firmly between palms of hands and roll frosted sides of cake in almonds until completely coated. Place on serving plate and spread remaining frosting on top of cake. Sprinkle remaining chopped almonds over top of cake. Refrigerate until ready to serve.

HINTS AND TIPS
To toast almonds, spread on a cookie sheet. Place in a 300°F oven and bake until lightly browned. Check frequently to prevent almonds from scorching. Remove from oven and let cool.

WINTER LEMON CAKE

SERVES 6 TO 8

CAKE
6 eggs, separated, room
   temperature
2 teaspoons grated lemon peel
2 tablespoons lemon juice
1 cup superfine sugar
½ teaspoon salt
1 cup cake flour

LEMON CREAM FILLING AND FROSTING
1½ cups sugar
½ cup sifted all-purpose flour
grated peel and juice of 2 lemons
2 eggs, beaten
2 cups heavy cream
crystallized orange and lemon slices

1. **Cake:** Preheat oven to 350°F. Grease three 8-inch round cake pans. Line bottoms of pans with waxed paper and grease the paper.

2. Beat egg yolks in mixing bowl at high speed about 5 minutes, or until thick and lemon-colored. Beat in lemon peel and juice until well blended. Add sugar and salt; continue beating at medium speed 6 to 7 minutes, or until very thick and smooth. Gradually add flour, one-fourth at a time, beating at low speed just until blended. Thoroughly wash the beaters.

3. Beat egg whites until stiff peaks form. Fold half of beaten whites into egg yolk mixture. Fold in remaining beaten whites until no white streaks remain. Divide batter equally among prepared pans and smooth tops.

4. Bake 20 to 25 minutes, or until tops are golden and cakes spring back when lightly pressed. Cool in pans on wire racks 5 minutes. Loosen edges of cakes with spatula and invert from pans onto racks. Remove pans, peel off waxed paper, and turn layers right side up. Cool completely.

5. **Lemon Cream Filling and Frosting:** Stir sugar and flour together in top of double boiler. Add enough water to lemon juice to measure 1¼ cups and add to sugar-flour mixture; add lemon peel and beaten eggs. Stir with wire whisk until mixture is smooth and no lumps remain. Set over simmering water and cook, stirring constantly, until mixture is thickened and comes to a boil. Remove from heat, pour into large bowl, and cool completely.

6. Beat cream until firm. Fold into cold lemon mixture. Refrigerate until needed.

7. To assemble and decorate cake, place 1 layer, bottom side up, on serving plate and spread with frosting. Top with second layer and spread with frosting. Place third layer on top. Spread remaining frosting over sides and top of cake, swirling decoratively. Refrigerate until ready to serve. Just before serving, decorate top of cake with crystallized orange and lemon slices.

HINTS AND TIPS
A sponge cake should have a very smooth, ungrainy texture. It is important that the sugar-egg yolk mixture be beaten until the sugar is completely dissolved. To test, rub a little of the mixture between your fingertips. If it feels grainy, continue beating until smooth.

SIMPLE JAM LAYER CAKE

SERVES 6 TO 8

½ cup butter or margarine,
  softened
1¼ cups granulated sugar
1 teaspoon vanilla
3 eggs
2 cups all-purpose flour
3 teaspoons baking powder
½ teaspoon salt
1 cup milk
¼ cup strawberry jam or favorite
  jam
confectioners sugar

1. Preheat oven to 350°F. Grease and flour two 8-inch round cake pans.

2. Cream butter in large mixing bowl until smooth. Add granulated sugar and beat until light and fluffy. Beat in vanilla. Add eggs, 1 at a time, beating well after each addition.

3. Stir flour, baking powder and salt together and add to creamed mixture alternately with milk, beating well after each addition, until well blended.

4. Pour batter into prepared pans and smooth tops. Bake 30 to 35 minutes, or until tops of cakes spring back when lightly pressed.

5. Cool in pans on wire racks 10 minutes. Invert from pans onto racks and cool completely.

6. Place 1 layer, bottom side up, on serving plate and spread with jam. Top with second layer. Sprinkle top with sifted confectioners sugar just before serving.

One-Bowl Method: Place ingredients, in order listed except jam and confectioners sugar, in large mixing bowl and beat at low speed until blended. Increase speed to high and beat 3 to 4 minutes, or until very smooth. Bake and assemble as directed above.

VARIATIONS
Chocolate Layer Cake: Increase sugar to 1½ cups. After adding eggs, beat in 3 squares (3 ounces) unsweetened chocolate, melted and cooled.
Whole-Wheat Layer Cake: Use ¾ cup granulated sugar and ½ cup firmly packed light brown sugar. Use 1 cup whole-wheat flour and 1 cup all-purpose flour.
Orange Layer Cake: Prepare as directed above, omitting vanilla. Add 1 to 2 teaspoons grated orange peel and substitute ½ cup orange juice for half the milk.
Lemon Layer Cake: Prepare as directed above, omitting vanilla. Beat 1 teaspoon grated lemon peel and 2 tablespoons lemon juice into creamed mixture.
Party Cupcakes: Prepare batter as directed above and pour into two 12-cup muffin pans lined with cupcake liners. Bake 18 to 20 minutes, or until toothpick inserted in center of a cupcake comes out clean. Cool in pans 5 minutes. Remove from pans and cool on wire racks. Frost and decorate as desired.

1. Cream butter until smooth. Add granulated sugar and beat until light and fluffy. Beat in vanilla. Add eggs, 1 at a time, beating well after each addition. Scrape sides of bowl occasionally with rubber spatula.

2. Bake 30 to 35 minutes, or until tops of cakes are golden and spring back when lightly pressed.

3. Place 1 layer, bottom side up, on serving plate and spread with jam. Top with second layer. Sprinkle with sifted confectioners sugar just before serving.

CHOCOLATE NUT TORTE

SERVES 8

CAKE
7 eggs, separated
1 cup sugar
1 teaspoon vanilla
1 cup ground hazelnuts
1 cup ground pecans
4 tablespoons plain dry bread
   crumbs
1 teaspoon baking powder
½ teaspoon salt

FILLING
1 cup heavy cream
2 tablespoons confectioners sugar
1 teaspoon vanilla
1 to 2 tablespoons brandy
   (optional)

FROSTING
4 squares (4 ounces) semisweet
   chocolate, broken into pieces
¼ cup butter or margarine
2 tablespoons instant coffee
   powder
2 teaspoons vanilla
4 cups confectioners sugar, sifted
whole hazelnuts or pecans

1. Cake: Place egg whites in large mixing bowl; let stand at room temperature 1 hour. Preheat oven to 375°F. Line bottoms of three 8-inch round cake pans with waxed or parchment paper. Grease sides of pans.

2. Beat egg yolks until thick and lemon-colored. Gradually beat in sugar and continue beating 3 minutes, or until thick. Beat in vanilla. Combine ground nuts, bread crumbs, baking powder and salt; fold into egg yolk mixture until thoroughly blended.

3. Beat egg whites until stiff peaks form. Stir half the beaten whites into egg yolk-nut mixture to lighten. Gradually fold in remaining beaten whites.

4. Divide mixture equally among prepared pans and smooth tops. Bake 25 minutes, or until tops of cakes spring back when lightly pressed. Cool in pans on wire racks 5 minutes. Remove pans from wire racks and cover racks with parchment paper or clean dish towel. Invert pans onto racks and cool cakes completely in pans.

5. Filling: Beat cream until thick. Add confectioners sugar and vanilla and beat until firm. Beat in brandy. Refrigerate until needed.

6. Frosting: Melt chocolate and butter together in top of double boiler. Remove from heat and cool. Dissolve coffee in 2 tablespoons hot water; stir into melted chocolate along with vanilla. Beat in confectioners sugar. Continue beating until frosting is good spreading consistency.

7. To assemble and decorate cake, run a spatula around edges of cooled cakes to loosen. Remove from pans and peel off paper. Trim off any crusty edges. Place 1 layer, bottom side up, on serving plate and spread with half of chilled filling. Top with second layer and spread with remaining filling. Top with third layer. Spread most of frosting over top and sides of cake with long, flat icing spatula. Spoon remaining frosting into pastry bag fitted with No. 2 star tip and pipe rosettes around top edge of cake. Decorate each rosette with whole hazelnut. Refrigerate at least 1 hour before serving to make cutting easy.

ORANGE-WALNUT CREAM GATEAU

SERVES 8 TO 10

CAKE
5 eggs, separated
1 cup sugar
2 teaspoons grated orange peel
¼ teaspoon salt
6 tablespoons orange juice
1 cup sifted cake flour

ORANGE BUTTERCREAM FROSTING
½ cup butter or margarine,
   softened
5 cups confectioners sugar
2 tablespoons milk or light cream
2 to 3 tablespoons orange juice
food coloring (optional)
½ cup finely chopped walnuts

DECORATION
thin slices candied orange peel or
   crystallized orange slices

1. Cake: Preheat oven to 350°F. Grease bottoms of two 9-inch round cake pans. Line bottoms with waxed paper and grease the paper.

2. Place egg yolks in mixing bowl and beat at medium speed about 5 minutes, or until thick and lemon-colored. Add ½ cup sugar, orange peel and salt; continue beating until very thick and fluffy.

3. Add orange juice and beat until well blended. Gradually beat in flour, one-fourth at a time, beating well after each addition, until well blended.

4. Beat egg whites until soft peaks form. Add remaining ½ cup sugar and continue beating until stiff peaks form. Fold beaten whites into egg yolk mixture.

5. Divide batter evenly between prepared pans and smooth tops. Bake 25 to 30 minutes, or until tops of cakes are golden and spring back when lightly pressed. Cool in pans on wire racks 10 minutes. Invert from pans onto racks, peel off waxed paper, and cool completely.

6. Orange Buttercream Frosting: Cream butter until light and fluffy. Gradually beat in confectioners sugar alternately with milk and orange juice. Continue beating until frosting is good spreading consistency. (Beat in a few drops of red and yellow food coloring if you want an orange-colored frosting.)

7. Cut each layer in half horizontally to make 4 layers. Place 1 layer, bottom side up, on serving plate lined with waxed paper strips (see page 48). Spread a little Orange Buttercream Frosting over cake layer. Top with second layer and spread with Frosting. Repeat until all layers have been filled. Spread remaining frosting over sides and top of cake, swirling decoratively with back of spoon. Lightly press chopped walnuts around sides of cake with small, flat-bladed spatula. Remove waxed paper strips. Decorate top of cake with thin slices of candied orange peel or crystallized orange slices. Refrigerate until ready to serve.

HINTS AND TIPS
To divide cakes into even layers, insert wooden toothpicks halfway up the sides of each layer all the way around. Using the toothpicks as your guide, slice through each cake layer with a long, sharp knife. Slide a thin piece of cardboard between the cut layers and gently lift off the top layer.

MAPLE SYRUP CAKE

SERVES 8

CAKE
2 cups all-purpose flour
3 teaspoons baking powder
2 teaspoons ground ginger
½ teaspoon cinnamon
½ teaspoon grated nutmeg
¼ teaspoon salt
½ cup butter or margarine, softened
¾ cup firmly packed light brown sugar
2 eggs
¾ cup maple syrup
½ cup milk

FILLING
1 cup heavy cream
confectioners sugar
½ cup finely chopped walnuts or pecans
2 tablespoons raisins

1. Cake: Preheat oven to 350°F. Grease and flour two 8-inch round cake pans.

2. Sift flour, baking powder, ginger, cinnamon, nutmeg and salt together; set aside.

3. Cream butter in mixing bowl until soft. Add brown sugar and beat until light and fluffy. Add eggs, 1 at a time, beating well after each addition. Gradually add maple syrup, beating constantly until well blended.

4. Add flour mixture alternately with milk, beating well after each addition, until well combined.

5. Divide batter equally between prepared pans and smooth tops.

6. Bake 25 to 30 minutes, or until toothpick inserted in center of each cake comes out clean. Cool in pans on wire racks 10 minutes. Invert from pans onto racks and cool completely.

7. Filling: Beat cream with 2 tablespoons confectioners sugar until firm. Fold in nuts and raisins. Place 1 cake layer, bottom side up, on serving plate and spread with filling. Top with second layer.

8. Cut 4 strips of waxed paper, 1-inch wide, and place strips across top of cake, spacing them evenly apart. Sift confectioners sugar over top of cake. Carefully remove the waxed paper strips, leaving stripes of sugar on cake. Refrigerate about 30 minutes before serving.

HINTS AND TIPS

The cake layers can be made ahead of time, cooled, tightly wrapped, and frozen until needed. To serve, thaw the layers, wrapped, at room temperature 2 to 3 hours. Prepare filling and assemble the cake. Refrigerate before serving.

ANGEL FOOD CAKE

SERVES 10 TO 12

CAKE
1 cup cake flour
1 cup confectioners sugar
1½ cups egg whites (about 12),
   room temperature
1½ teaspoons cream of tartar
2 teaspoons vanilla
½ teaspoon salt
½ teaspoon almond extract
   (optional)
¾ cup granulated or superfine
   sugar

ORANGE RUM SAUCE
¼ cup sugar
1 tablespoon cornstarch
1½ cups orange juice
1 tablespoon lemon juice
1 tablespoon grated orange peel
1 egg yolk, beaten
2 tablespoons butter or margarine
1 to 2 tablespoons rum

1. Cake: Preheat oven to 375°F. Sift flour and confectioners sugar onto sheet of waxed paper. Spoon mixture back into sifter and sift 3 more times; set aside.

2. Place egg whites in large mixing bowl and add cream of tartar; beat at medium speed until frothy. Beat in vanilla, salt and almond extract. Continue beating at medium speed until soft peaks form. Gradually beat in granulated sugar, 2 tablespoons at a time, beating at high speed, until stiff peaks form and sugar is completely dissolved.

3. Sift about one-fourth of flour mixture over beaten whites and fold in with rubber spatula just until blended. Repeat until all flour mixture has been added.

4. Pour batter into ungreased 10-inch tube pan. Gently cut through batter with long, thin metal spatula to break up any air pockets.

5. Bake in center of oven 35 to 40 minutes, or until top of cake springs back when lightly pressed. (Any cracks on top of cake should look and feel dry.) Remove cake from oven and immediately invert pan over neck of soda bottle or funnel (unless pan has legs) and cool completely in pan. To remove from pan, loosen edges with metal spatula. Invert onto serving plate, gently tapping and shaking pan to remove cake. Brush away any loose crumbs.

6. Orange-Rum Sauce: Stir sugar and cornstarch together in saucepan. Add orange and lemon juices, orange peel, and ½ cup water; stir with wire whisk until well blended. Place over low heat and cook, stirring constantly, until mixture comes to a boil and is slightly thickened. Remove from heat and add a small amount of sauce to beaten egg yolk, stirring constantly. Pour mixture back into pan, return to low heat, and cook, stirring constantly, about 1 to 2 minutes, or until slightly thickened. Remove from heat and stir in butter until melted. Let cool and stir in rum. Serve warm or chilled, spooned over slices of Angel Food Cake.

VARIATION
Chocolate Angel Food Cake: Substitute ¼ cup unsweetened cocoa for ¼ cup of the cake flour. Sift cocoa, flour and confectioners sugar together 3 times.

CHOCOLATE-ALMOND CAKE

SERVES 6 TO 8

CAKE
6 eggs, separated
¾ cup sugar
¼ teaspoon salt
grated peel of 1 orange
¾ cup sifted all-purpose flour
¼ cup unsweetened cocoa

CHOCOLATE FROSTING
1 egg
⅔ cup sugar
2 tablespoons unsweetened cocoa
¼ cup all-purpose flour
1½ cups heavy cream
¾ cup toasted chopped almonds
1 cup sweetened whipped cream
  (optional)
grated semisweet chocolate
  (optional)

1. Cake: Preheat oven to 350°F. Grease and flour three 8-inch round cake pans.

2. Beat egg yolks, sugar and salt together about 6 minutes, or until light and fluffy. Beat in orange peel.

3. Sift flour and cocoa together and gradually fold into egg yolk mixture until thoroughly combined. Thoroughly wash the beaters.

4. Beat egg whites until stiff peaks form. Stir about 1 cup beaten whites into egg yolk-flour mixture to lighten. Fold in remaining beaten whites until no white streaks remain.

5. Divide batter equally among prepared pans and smooth tops. Bake 25 to 30 minutes, or until cakes shrink away from sides of pans and tops spring back when lightly pressed. Cool in pans on wire racks 5 minutes. Invert from pans onto racks and turn cakes right side up to cool completely.

6. Chocolate Frosting: Beat egg and sugar together until foamy. Stir cocoa and flour together in small bowl, add ⅔ cup water, and stir until well blended and smooth. Pour into egg-sugar mixture and stir until thoroughly combined. Pour into saucepan and cook over low heat, stirring constantly, until smooth and very thick. Remove from heat and cool completely. Beat cream until firm and fold into cooled cocoa mixture.

7. Place 1 cake layer on clean work surface and spread with one-fourth of Chocolate Frosting. Top with second layer and spread with one-fourth of frosting. Top with remaining layer. Spread half of remaining frosting around sides of cake. Sprinkle almonds on a sheet of waxed paper. Hold cake firmly between palms of hands and roll frosted sides of cake in almonds until completely coated. Place cake on serving plate. Spread remaining frosting over top. Decorate top by drawing tip of small, flat spatula from outside of cake in toward center. If desired, pipe whipped cream rosettes or swirls around outside edge of cake. Just before serving, dust rosettes with grated chocolate.

ELEGANT ORANGE BLOSSOM CAKE

SERVES 8 TO 10

CAKE
2¼ cups cake flour
2½ teaspoons baking powder
½ teaspoon salt
¾ cup butter or margarine,
    softened
1½ cups sugar
1 tablespoon grated orange peel
4 eggs
¾ cup orange juice

CREAMY ORANGE BUTTER FROSTING
½ cup light corn syrup
3 egg yolks
1 cup sweet butter, softened
1 tablespoon orange flower water
red and yellow food coloring
    (optional)
½ cup sliced blanched almonds,
    toasted

ORANGE GLACÉ ICING
1½ cups confectioners sugar,
    sifted
1 tablespoon orange flower water
red and yellow food coloring
    (optional)

1. Cake: Preheat oven to 350°F. Grease and flour two 9-inch round cake pans.

2. Sift flour, baking powder and salt together; set aside. Cream butter and sugar in large mixing bowl until light and fluffy. Beat in orange peel. Add eggs, 1 at a time, beating well after each addition. Add flour mixture alternately with orange juice, beating at low speed after each addition, until well blended.

3. Divide batter equally between prepared pans and smooth tops. Bake 25 to 30 minutes, or until toothpick inserted in center of each cake comes out clean. Cool in pans on wire racks 10 minutes. Invert from pans onto racks and cool completely.

4. Creamy Orange Butter Frosting: Place corn syrup in saucepan and bring to a boil. Set candy thermometer in syrup and gently boil 5 minutes, or until temperature registers 230°F to 234°F (soft ball stage). Remove from heat. Beat egg yolks in bowl until smooth. Gradually add hot syrup to egg yolks, pouring in thin, steady stream, beating constantly. Continue to beat until thick and thoroughly cooled.

5. Beat butter until fluffy. Add egg yolk-syrup mixture slowly, beating until smooth. Beat in orange flower water and a few drops of food coloring to tint frosting. Spoon scant 1 cup frosting into pastry bag fitted with open star tip. Refrigerate until needed. Chill remaining frosting a few minutes to give it good spreading consistency.

6. To assemble and decorate cake, place 1 layer, bottom side up, on clean work surface and spread with half the chilled frosting. Top with second layer. Spread remaining frosting around sides of cake.

7. Scatter almonds on sheet of waxed paper. Hold cake firmly between palms of hands and roll frosted sides of cake in almonds until coated. Place on serving plate.

8. Orange Glacé Icing: Stir confectioners sugar, orange flower water and 1 to 2 teaspoons hot water together until fairly thick and smooth. Add a few drops of food coloring, if desired. Pour Orange Glacé Icing over top of cake and spread to edges with icing spatula. Let stand until icing is set.

9. Pipe a row of shells or rosettes around top edge of cake with reserved Creamy Orange Butter Frosting. Refrigerate until ready to serve.

FROSTED WALNUT LAYER CAKE

SERVES 6 TO 8

CAKE
2 cups all-purpose flour
2 teaspoons baking powder
½ teaspoon salt
¾ cup butter or margarine,
    softened
1½ cups firmly packed light brown
    sugar
3 eggs
2 teaspoons instant coffee powder
¾ cup warm milk
½ cup finely chopped walnuts

SEVEN MINUTE FROSTING
2 egg whites
1½ cups sugar
¼ teaspoon cream of tartar
½ teaspoon vanilla

DECORATION
walnut halves

1. Cake: Preheat oven to 350°F. Grease deep 8-inch round cake pan or springform pan. Line bottom of pan with waxed paper and grease the paper.

2. Sift flour, baking powder and salt together; set aside. Cream butter in large mixing bowl until soft. Beat in brown sugar until light and fluffy. Add eggs, 1 at a time, beating well after each addition.

3. Dissolve coffee in milk. Add flour mixture alternately with coffee mixture to creamed mixture, beating well after each addition. Stir in walnuts until well blended. Spread batter in prepared pan.

4. Bake 1 hour to 1 hour 10 minutes, or until cake tester inserted in center comes out clean. Cool in pan on wire rack 10 minutes. Invert from pan onto rack, peel off waxed paper, and cool completely. When cool, cut cake horizontally into 3 layers. (See page 38.)

5. Seven Minute Frosting: Place egg whites, sugar, cream of tartar, vanilla and ¼ cup water in top of double boiler; beat at medium speed 1 minute. Set over simmering water and beat 7 minutes, or until soft peaks form. Remove from heat and continue beating until frosting is thick and fluffy. Use to frost cake immediately.

6. Place 1 cake layer on serving plate and spread with about one-fourth of frosting. Top with second layer and spread with one-fourth of remaining frosting. Top with third layer. Spread remaining frosting over sides and top of cake, smoothing sides with flat-bladed knife or icing spatula. Decorate top with walnut halves.

HINTS AND TIPS

To frost a cake neatly, place 1 cake layer in the center of the plate. Cut four strips of waxed paper and slip the strips of waxed paper under the layer to cover the edge of the plate. Frost the cake completely, letting the excess frosting run onto the waxed paper. Let the frosted cake stand about 10 minutes, then pull out each strip of waxed paper quickly. The plate will remain clean.

STRAWBERRY CREAM CAKE

SERVES 6 TO 8

CAKE
4 eggs
½ cup sugar
1 teaspoon vanilla
¾ cup all-purpose flour, sifted
   twice
¼ cup sweet butter, melted and
   cooled
3 tablespoons kirsch

WHIPPED CREAM FILLING AND FROSTING
2 pints strawberries
2 cups heavy cream
½ cup confectioners sugar
1½ teaspoons vanilla or 1 teaspoon
   vanilla and ½ teaspoon almond
   extract
¾ cup sliced blanched almonds,
   toasted

1. Cake: Preheat oven to 350°F. Grease three 8-inch round cake pans. Line bottoms of pans with waxed paper and grease and flour the paper and sides of pan.

2. Place eggs in large mixing bowl set over pan of very hot water. (Do not let bottom of bowl touch water.) Let stand about 5 to 6 minutes, or until eggs are warm to the touch. Beat eggs at high speed until fluffy. Gradually beat in sugar. Continue beating about 10 to 12 minutes, or until egg mixture falls from beaters in thick, glossy ribbons. Beat in vanilla. Remove bowl from pan of water.

3. Sprinkle one-fourth of flour over beaten egg mixture and fold in with rubber spatula. Repeat until all of flour has been added. Fold in butter until blended and streaks disappear.

4. Divide batter equally among prepared pans and smooth tops. Bake 18 to 20 minutes, or until tops of cakes spring back when lightly pressed. Cool in pans on wire racks 5 minutes. Loosen edges of cakes from pans with metal spatula and invert from pans onto racks. Peel off waxed paper and cool completely.

5. When layers are cool, prick each layer all over with a fork and sprinkle each layer with 1 tablespoon kirsch.

6. Whipped Cream Filling and Frosting: Wash and hull strawberries, reserving 5 for decoration. Thickly slice remaining strawberries and set aside. Beat cream until thick. Add confectioners sugar and vanilla; continue beating until firm.

7. Place 1 cake layer on serving plate and spread with one-fourth of whipped cream. Arrange half of sliced strawberries on top of whipped cream. Top with a second cake layer, spread with one-fourth of remaining whipped cream and arrange remaining sliced strawberries over whipped cream. Top with remaining cake layer. Spoon about ¾ cup of remaining whipped cream into pastry bag fitted with star tip and set aside in refrigerator. Spread remaining whipped cream over sides and top of cake, smoothing with long, flat icing spatula.

8. Press almonds around the sides of cake. Cut reserved strawberries in half and arrange in a circle, cut side down, on top of cake. Pipe reserved whipped cream in swirls or rosettes around the top edge of cake and in the center. Refrigerate until ready to serve.

51

ALMOND-MOCHA RUM TORTE

SERVES 12

CAKE
4 squares (4 ounces) semisweet chocolate, coarsely chopped
6 tablespoons dark rum
½ cup sweet butter
¾ cup sugar
3 eggs, separated
¾ teaspoon almond extract
½ cup ground almonds
½ cup sifted cake flour

BUTTERCREAM FROSTING
6 tablespoons butter or margarine, softened
3 cups sifted confectioners sugar
1 egg yolk
1 teaspoon vanilla
1 tablespoon instant coffee powder
6 squares (6 ounces) semisweet chocolate, chopped

1. Cake: Preheat oven to 350°F. Grease and flour 9-inch springform pan.

2. Melt chocolate in top of double boiler. Remove from heat and let cool. Stir in 4 tablespoons rum until smooth and well blended; set aside.

3. Cream butter and sugar in mixing bowl until light and fluffy. Add egg yolks, 1 at a time, beating well after each addition. Beat in cooled chocolate-rum mixture until well blended. Fold in almond extract and ground almonds. Gradually fold in flour until blended.

4. Beat egg whites until stiff peaks form. Stir half the beaten whites into batter to lighten. Fold in remaining beaten whites.

5. Pour batter into prepared pan and smooth top. Bake 35 to 40 minutes, or until cake tester inserted in center comes out clean. Cool in pan on wire rack 10 minutes. Invert from pan onto rack and cool completely. When cool, place cake on serving plate and prick top of cake all over with a fork. Sprinkle with remaining 2 tablespoons rum; let stand about 2 hours.

6. Buttercream Frosting: Beat butter until very light and fluffy. Gradually beat in confectioners sugar until well blended. Beat in egg yolk. Continue beating until frosting is good spreading consistency. Measure scant 1 cup frosting, place in a separate bowl and beat in vanilla; refrigerate. Dissolve coffee in 1 tablespoon hot water and cool. Beat into unflavored frosting until well blended; refrigerate.

7. Draw an 8-inch circle on a sheet of parchment paper. Melt chocolate in top of double boiler. Pour melted chocolate into center of circle and spread it evenly within circle, about ¼ inch thick. Let stand until chocolate is firm.

8. Spread coffee-flavored frosting over sides and top of the cake, smoothing with icing spatula.

9. Cut firm chocolate into 12 pie-shaped wedges. Arrange chocolate wedges upright on top of cake, spacing chocolate evenly. Lightly press into frosting.

10. Spoon vanilla-flavored frosting into pastry bag fitted with medium-size star tip. Pipe vanilla-flavored frosting in a border around bottom edge of cake and pipe a small swirl or rosette between each chocolate wedge and in center of cake.

BOSTON CREAM PIE

SERVES 6 TO 8

CAKE
1 cup cake flour
1 teaspoon baking powder
¼ teaspoon salt
3 eggs
1 cup sugar
1 tablespoon lemon juice
1 teaspoon grated lemon peel
6 tablespoons hot milk

CREAM FILLING
⅓ cup sugar
2 tablespoons cornstarch
¼ teaspoon salt
1½ cups milk or light cream
3 egg yolks
1 tablespoon butter or margarine
2 teaspoons vanilla

CHOCOLATE GLAZE
3 squares (3 ounces) unsweetened
   chocolate, broken into pieces
3 tablespoons butter or margarine
1 cup confectioners sugar, sifted
1 teaspoon vanilla

1. Cake: Preheat oven to 350°F. Grease two 8-inch round cake pans. Line bottoms of pans with waxed paper and grease the paper.

2. Sift flour, baking powder and salt together; set aside.

3. Beat eggs in mixing bowl until thick and lemon-colored. Gradually beat in sugar and continue beating until very thick. Beat in lemon juice and peel. Gradually fold in flour mixture until thoroughly blended. Add hot milk slowly and stir just until blended and smooth.

4. Divide batter equally between prepared pans and smooth tops. Bake 25 to 30 minutes, or until tops spring back when lightly pressed. Cool in pans on wire racks 10 minutes. Invert from pans onto racks, peel off waxed paper, and cool completely.

5. Cream Filling: Stir sugar, cornstarch and salt together in small saucepan. Add milk and stir with wire whisk until mixture is well blended and no lumps remain. Place over low heat and cook, stirring constantly, until mixture is thickened and comes to a boil. Remove from heat. Beat egg yolks in small bowl. Stir in 4 tablespoons hot milk mixture until well blended. Slowly pour egg yolk mixture back into saucepan. Return to low heat and cook, stirring constantly, until thickened (don't let mixture come to a boil). Remove from heat and let cool slightly. Add butter and stir until melted. Stir in vanilla. Press a piece of waxed paper over surface of filling and refrigerate until needed.

6. Chocolate Glaze: Melt chocolate and butter in top of double boiler. Remove from heat and stir in confectioners sugar and vanilla. Stir in 1 to 2 tablespoons hot water until glaze is smooth and shiny.

7. To assemble cake, place 1 layer, bottom side up, on serving plate and spread with Cream Filling. Top with second layer. Spread Chocolate Glaze over top of cake. Let stand until glaze is set before serving.

RICH CHOCOLATE CREAM SLICE

SERVES 8 TO 10

CAKE
4 squares (4 ounces) semisweet
   chocolate
½ cup butter, softened
½ cup sugar
4 eggs, separated
½ cup all-purpose flour, sifted

CHOCOLATE FILLING
6 squares (6 ounces) semisweet
   chocolate, coarsely chopped
¾ cup heavy cream
¼ cup sugar
½ teaspoon vanilla
2 tablespoons chocolate-flavored
   liqueur

CHOCOLATE GLAZE
½ cup sugar
4 squares (4 ounces) semisweet
   chocolate
1 tablespoon butter

1. Cake: Preheat oven to 350°F. Grease 9 × 5-inch loaf pan. Melt chocolate in top of double boiler over low heat. Remove from heat; set aside to cool.

2. Cream butter and sugar in medium-size mixing bowl until light and fluffy. Beat in melted chocolate until well blended. Add egg yolks, one at a time, beating well after each addition; set aside. Wash and dry beaters thoroughly.

3. Beat egg whites in separate bowl until firm. Stir 2 tablespoons beaten egg whites into chocolate mixture to lighten. Sprinkle flour over chocolate mixture and fold in until thoroughly blended. Fold in remaining egg whites until no white streaks remain.

4. Spread batter evenly in prepared pan. Bake 35 to 40 minutes or until cake tester inserted in center of cake comes out clean.

5. Cool cake in pan on wire rack 15 minutes. Run knife around edges of cake to loosen. Invert cake on rack, remove pan and let cake cool completely.

6. Filling: Place chocolate, cream and sugar in heavy saucepan. Place over low heat and cook, stirring constantly, until chocolate is melted and sugar dissolved. Pour mixture into bowl and let stand 15 minutes at room temperature; refrigerate 1 hour.

7. Remove filling from refrigerator and beat in vanilla and liqueur at medium speed until mixture is firm. (If necessary, return to refrigerator for 10 minutes to give it good spreading consistency.)

8. Keeping cake on wire rack, cut horizontally through center to make 2 layers. Spread chocolate filling evenly over bottom half of cake with long, flat spatula. Place top half of cake over filling. Refrigerate on rack 1 hour.

9. Glaze: Place sugar, chocolate and 3 tablespoons water in heavy saucepan. Cook over low heat, stirring constantly, until chocolate is melted and sugar dissolved. Remove from heat and stir in butter until melted. Remove cake from refrigerator. Set cake, still on rack, over cookie sheet. Pour glaze over top of cake and spread evenly with long, flat spatula. Allow glaze to run down sides of cake to cover cake completely. Let stand 5 minutes.

10. Slide wide spatula under cake carefully and lift off rack. Place cake on serving plate and refrigerate 20 minutes or until glaze is firm. Cut cake into thick slices with long, sharp knife.

CHEESECAKES AND MERINGUES

Three kinds of special cakes are included in this chapter: refrigerator cheesecakes, baked cheesecakes, and cakes that feature meringue. There are a few techniques that should be understood before these are undertaken. Once they're mastered, you can make these cakes with confidence. Read the hints and tips that follow before you start baking to insure success with the recipes that follow.

HINTS AND TIPS FOR HANDLING GELATIN

● It is important to dissolve gelatin completely before combining it with other ingredients. If it is not properly dissolved, your cheesecake will not set properly and the texture will be grainy.
● Measure liquid that is added to a gelatin mixture carefully. If you add too much liquid, your cheesecake will not set properly. If you don't add enough liquid, the cake will have a heavy texture.
● Don't allow a gelatin mixture to set firmly before folding in beaten egg whites or whipped cream. It should be removed from the refrigerator when it has thickened, but not set.

HINTS AND TIPS FOR BEATING EGG WHITES

● Separate eggs while they are still cold. Allow whites to come to room temperature before beating in order to get maximum volume.
● Be sure your mixing bowl and beaters are thoroughly clean. Even the slightest amount of grease, liquid or egg yolk can prevent egg whites from stiffening satisfactorily.
● Add cream of tartar to egg whites as you begin to beat them OR beat egg whites in a copper bowl. It is not necessary to add cream of tartar when you use a copper bowl.
● Beat egg whites just before you are ready to fold them into the other ingredients. If beaten egg whites are allowed to stand, they will lose volume that can never be regained.
● When egg whites are at the soft peak stage, the tip of the peak will flop over. When egg whites reach the stiff peak stage, the peaks stand up straight when the beater is lifted, and when the bowl is turned upside-down, the beaten whites don't fall out.

HINTS AND TIPS FOR MAKING MERINGUES

● Meringues are made with beaten egg whites (see above) and sugar. Vanilla or other flavoring is added as desired.
● Sugar is added to beaten egg whites 1 tablespoon at a time. It is important to be sure each spoonful has been dissolved before more sugar is added. Beat until mixture stands in stiff, glossy peaks. Rub a little meringue between your fingertips. If it feels grainy, continue beating until smooth.
● When meringues are baked they must be allowed to remain in a warm oven that has been turned off until they are dry. Then they must be cooled completely on a cookie sheet.
● Don't try to make meringues on a humid day.
● Store cooled meringues immediately in an airtight container, otherwise the meringues will disintegrate.

Continued

Clockwise: Strawberry Cheesecake (page 60), Chocolate Baked Alaska (page 76), Chocolate Mousse Cheesecake (page 61)

HINTS AND TIPS ABOUT FOLDING

● Stirring and folding are two entirely different techniques. If you stir whipped cream or beaten egg whites into a mixture, the air that has been beaten into them will be lost and the volume will be reduced.

● Always fold the egg whites or whipped cream into the other ingredients. Don't fold a heavy base into the egg whites or whipped cream because you will lose volume.

● To fold properly, spoon a small amount (1 or 2 tablespoons) of beaten egg white or whipped cream into the other ingredients. Stir well to lighten the mixture. Then spoon the remainder of the egg whites or whipped cream on top of the lightened mixture. Use a rubber spatula and make circular "down-up-over" motions. Turn the bowl with the other hand as you fold.

STRAWBERRY CHEESECAKE

SERVES 8 TO 10

CRUST
1 cup shortbread cookie crumbs
1 tablespoon sugar
3 tablespoons butter or margarine, melted

FILLING
1 pint strawberries
2 teaspoons grated orange peel
2 tablespoons orange juice
4 teaspoons unflavored gelatin (about 1½ envelopes)
¼ cup boiling water
1 cup cottage cheese
¾ cup sugar
1 teaspoon vanilla
½ cup plain yogurt
1 cup heavy cream
1 egg white

1. Crust: Preheat oven to 350°F. Grease 8-inch springform pan. Combine cookie crumbs and sugar. Pour in melted butter and stir until blended. Press crumb mixture onto bottom of prepared pan. Bake 8 to 10 minutes. Remove from oven and cool on wire rack.

2. Filling: Wash and hull strawberries, reserving 6 for decoration. Slice remaining strawberries and place in container of food processor or blender. Add orange peel and juice. Process until puréed; set aside. Sprinkle gelatin over boiling water and stir until dissolved; cool.

3. Beat cottage cheese until almost smooth. Gradually beat in sugar, vanilla, yogurt and puréed strawberries. Beat in gelatin mixture. Beat cream until very thick, but not stiff. Fold whipped cream into strawberry mixture. Beat egg white until stiff peaks form and fold in. Pour mixture over cooled crust and smooth top. Refrigerate 4 hours, or until set.

4. To serve, carefully run tip of sharp knife around inside edge of pan and release side of pan. Place cake on serving plate. Cut reserved strawberries in half and arrange on cake to decorate.

Picture, see page 58

CHOCOLATE MOUSSE CHEESECAKE

SERVES 10 TO 12

CRUST
1 cup graham cracker crumbs
2 tablespoons unsweetened cocoa
3 tablespoons sugar
4 tablespoons butter, melted

FILLING
6 squares (6 ounces) semisweet
  chocolate
1 envelope unflavored gelatin
¼ cup warm milk or water
1 package (8 ounces) cream
  cheese, softened
½ cup granulated sugar
1 teaspoon almond extract or
  2 teaspoons vanilla
3 eggs, separated
¼ cup confectioners sugar
1 cup heavy cream
grated chocolate or sweetened
  whipped cream

1. **Crust:** Preheat oven to 350°F. Grease 8-inch springform pan. Stir graham cracker crumbs, cocoa and sugar together in bowl until combined. Stir in butter until well blended. Press crumb mixture onto bottom of prepared pan, smoothing to an even thickness. Bake 10 minutes. Remove from oven and cool completely on wire rack.

2. **Filling:** Melt chocolate in top of double boiler. Remove from heat and cool completely. Sprinkle gelatin over warm milk, stir well, and let stand 5 minutes. Beat cream cheese in mixing bowl until fluffy. Beat in granulated sugar and almond extract until light and fluffy. Add egg yolks, 1 at a time, beating well after each addition. Add cooled chocolate and gelatin mixture and beat until well combined; set aside. Thoroughly wash the beaters.

3. Beat egg whites until foamy. Beat in confectioners sugar until stiff peaks form. Fold beaten whites into chocolate mixture. Beat cream until thick, but not stiff. Fold into chocolate mixture. Pour mixture over cooled crust and smooth top. Refrigerate 4 hours, or until set.

4. To serve, carefully run tip of sharp knife around inside edge of pan and release side of pan. Slip wide spatula under crust and slide cheesecake onto serving plate. Decorate top with grated chocolate or sweetened whipped cream.

Picture, see page 58

VARIATION
Mocha Mousse Cheesecake: Substitute ¼ cup hot strong black coffee for warm milk. Dissolve gelatin in coffee and proceed as directed above.

HINTS AND TIPS
To make the crust in a food processor, break 8 whole graham crackers into pieces and place in bowl of food processor fitted with chopping blade. Process to fine crumbs. Add the cocoa and sugar and process about 5 seconds to blend. Cut unmelted butter into 4 or 5 pieces and add to the bowl. Process until well blended.

CHERRY-TOPPED CHEESECAKE

SERVES 10 TO 12

CRUST
1 cup graham cracker crumbs
2 tablespoons sugar
4 tablespoons butter or margarine,
  melted

FILLING
2 cups cottage cheese
¾ cup sugar
3 eggs, separated
1 teaspoon vanilla
grated peel of 1 lemon
grated peel of 1 orange
½ cup heavy cream
⅓ cup all-purpose flour, sifted

CHERRY TOPPING
1 can (16 ounces) dark sweet
  cherries
4 teaspoons cornstarch
1 tablespoon granulated sugar
1 teaspoon lemon juice
1 tablespoon kirsch (optional)
½ cup heavy cream
2 tablespoons confectioners sugar

1. Crust: Preheat oven to 350°F. Grease 9-inch springform pan. Stir graham cracker crumbs and sugar together in small bowl. Pour in melted butter and stir until well blended. Press crumb mixture evenly onto bottom of prepared pan. Bake 10 minutes. Remove from oven and cool completely on wire rack. Lower oven temperature to 300°F.

2. Filling: Place cottage cheese in strainer and press out any excess liquid with back of spoon. Place in large mixing bowl and beat until almost smooth. Beat in sugar until light. Add egg yolks, 1 at a time, beating well after each addition. Add vanilla, and lemon and orange peels, beating until well blended. Beat in cream just until mixed. Sprinkle with flour and beat until well blended. Thoroughly wash the beaters.

3. Beat egg whites in separate bowl until stiff peaks form. Fold beaten whites into cottage cheese mixture. Pour mixture over cooled crust and smooth top. Bake 1 hour to 1 hour 10 minutes, or until center is firm. Cool completely in pan on wire rack. Refrigerate in pan 3 hours.

4. Cherry Topping: Drain cherries, reserving syrup. Stir cornstarch and granulated sugar together in saucepan. Stir in lemon juice and reserved cherry syrup until well blended. Place over low heat and cook, stirring constantly, until mixture comes to a boil and thickens. Remove from heat and let stand 3 minutes to cool slightly. Stir in kirsch. Add cherries and stir gently with wooden spoon. Cool to room temperature. Spoon cherry mixture over cheesecake to within 1 inch of outside edge. Refrigerate until topping is set.

5. To serve, remove side of pan and place cheesecake on serving plate. Beat cream with confectioners sugar until stiff. Spoon into pastry bag fitted with star tip and pipe around edge of cheesecake.

HINTS AND TIPS
Instead of beating cottage cheese with an electric mixer, place in blender or food processor and process about 10 seconds. You will get smoother cottage cheese this way and cake will be less grainy.

SOUR CREAM-LEMON CHEESECAKE

SERVES 8 TO 10

CRUST
1 cup zwieback cookie crumbs
2 tablespoons sugar
½ teaspoon ground allspice
3 tablespoons butter or margarine,
  melted

FILLING
2 envelopes unflavored gelatin
3 egg yolks
⅔ cup sugar
1 package (8 ounces) cream
  cheese, softened
1 cup cottage cheese
¼ cup lemon juice
2 teaspoons grated lemon peel
1 teaspoon vanilla
2 cups dairy sour cream
fresh raspberries, blueberries or
  strawberries

1. **Crust:** Preheat oven to 350°F. Grease 8-inch springform pan. Combine cookie crumbs, sugar and allspice in small bowl. Pour in melted butter and stir until well blended. Press crumb mixture onto bottom of prepared pan. Bake 8 to 10 minutes. Remove from oven and cool completely on wire rack.

2. **Filling:** Sprinkle gelatin over ¼ cup cold water, stir to dissolve, and set aside.

3. Beat egg yolks and sugar together in top of double boiler until thick and lemon-colored. Place over simmering water and cook, stirring constantly, until sugar is dissolved and mixture is thickened. Stir in softened gelatin and cook, stirring constantly, until gelatin is completely dissolved and mixture is thickened. Remove from heat; cool completely.

4. Beat cream cheese and cottage cheese together in large mixing bowl until almost smooth. Add lemon juice, lemon peel and vanilla; beat until well blended. Gradually beat in cooled gelatin mixture until thoroughly combined. Stir in sour cream until well blended. Pour mixture over cooled crust and smooth top. Refrigerate 4 hours, or until set.

5. To serve, carefully run tip of sharp knife around inside edge of pan and release side of pan. Place cheesecake on serving plate. Arrange fresh fruit decoratively on top.

HINTS AND TIPS
Process zwieback cookies in a food processor to make crumbs quickly. Measure the crumbs, return them to the container of the food processor and add the remaining crust ingredients for quick and efficient mixing.

NO-BAKE SWIRLED CHEESECAKE

SERVES 10 TO 12

CRUST
1¾ cups chocolate wafer cookie
    crumbs
2 tablespoons sugar
6 tablespoons butter or margarine,
    melted

FILLING
1 cup cottage cheese
1 package (8 ounces) cream
    cheese, softened
⅔ cup sugar
1 teaspoon vanilla
1 envelope unflavored gelatin
1 cup heavy cream
2 egg whites
1 bar (4 ounces) sweet chocolate
1 tablespoon butter
2 tablespoons milk

DECORATION
1 can (11 ounces) mandarin orange
    sections, well drained

1. Crust: Preheat oven to 350°F. Grease 9-inch springform pan. Combine cookie crumbs and sugar in bowl. Pour in melted butter and stir until well blended. Press crumb mixture onto bottom and halfway up sides of prepared pan. Bake 10 to 12 minutes. Remove from oven and cool completely on wire racks.

2. Filling: Place cottage cheese in fine strainer and press out any excess liquid with back of spoon. Place in large mixing bowl and beat until almost smooth. Add cream cheese and beat until smooth. Beat in sugar and vanilla.

3. Sprinkle gelatin over cream in small saucepan. Place over low heat and cook, stirring constantly, until gelatin is dissolved. Remove from heat and cool completely. Gradually add cooled gelatin mixture to cottage cheese mixture, beating constantly until blended; set aside. Thoroughly wash the beaters.

4. Beat egg whites until stiff peaks form and fold into cottage cheese mixture. Refrigerate until mixture is thickened and mounds form when dropped from a spoon.

5. Place chocolate, butter and milk in small saucepan over low heat, stirring until melted and smooth. Remove from heat and cool completely.

6. Remove 1 cup of thickened cottage cheese mixture and place in separate bowl. Beat in melted chocolate mixture until well blended. Pour remaining cottage cheese mixture into cooled crust. Slowly pour chocolate mixture, in zig-zag fashion, over top of cheesecake. Swirl chocolate mixture through cheesecake, using small flat bladed knife to achieve marbled effect. Refrigerate 4 hours, or until set.

7. To serve, carefully release side of pan and place cheesecake on serving plate. Arrange mandarin oranges around outside edge.

HINTS AND TIPS
To remove cheesecake from bottom of pan, slide a wide spatula between bottom of cheesecake and pan and carefully lift cheesecake onto a serving plate.

CLASSIC BAKED CHEESECAKE

SERVES 10 TO 12

CRUST
1½ cups graham cracker crumbs
2 tablespoons sugar
5 tablespoons butter or margarine, melted

FILLING
4 packages (8 ounces each) cream cheese, softened
1¼ cups sugar
4 eggs, beaten
2 teaspoons vanilla or 1 teaspoon vanilla and 1 teaspoon almond extract
grated peel of 1 lemon
2 tablespoons lemon juice
¼ cup all-purpose flour
¼ cup heavy cream
1 cup dairy sour cream

1. **Crust:** Preheat oven to 350°F. Grease 9-inch springform pan. Combine graham cracker crumbs and sugar in bowl. Pour in melted butter and stir until well blended. Press crumb mixture onto bottom and partially up sides of prepared pan. Bake 10 minutes. Remove from oven and cool completely on wire rack. Raise temperature to 450°F.

2. **Filling:** Beat cream cheese in large mixing bowl until smooth. Add sugar and beat until light and fluffy. Beat in eggs, vanilla, lemon peel and juice. Sprinkle flour over cream cheese mixture and beat just until blended. Add heavy cream and sour cream; stir until well blended.

3. Pour cream cheese mixture into cooled crust and smooth top. Bake 45 to 50 minutes, or until edges are lightly browned and center is almost set. Turn off oven and open oven door. Leave cheesecake in oven 2 hours to cool.

4. Remove from oven and cool completely in pan on wire rack. Refrigerate several hours before serving. Remove from pan and serve topped with fresh strawberries, blueberries or raspberries.

PINEAPPLE-CHEESE PIE

SERVES 8

CRUST
1½ cups graham cracker crumbs
3 tablespoons sugar
5 tablespoons butter or margarine, melted

FILLING
2 packages (8 ounces each) cream cheese, softened
⅔ cup sugar
2 eggs, beaten
1 teaspoon vanilla
½ cup dairy sour cream

TOPPING
1 can (20 ounces) crushed pineapple, undrained
1 tablespoon cornstarch
1 tablespoon lemon juice
1 teaspoon butter or margarine

1. **Crust:** Preheat oven to 350°F. Grease 9-inch pie plate. Combine graham cracker crumbs and sugar in bowl. Pour in melted butter and stir until well blended. Press crumb mixture onto bottom and up sides of prepared pie plate, making rim at top edge of pie plate; set aside.

2. **Filling:** Beat cream cheese in bowl until smooth. Add sugar and beat until light and fluffy. Add eggs, vanilla and sour cream; beat until smooth. Pour cream cheese mixture into prepared crust.

3. Bake 30 to 35 minutes, or until center is set. Remove from oven and cool completely on wire rack.

4. **Topping:** Place pineapple with liquid and cornstarch in heavy saucepan over medium heat. Cook, stirring constantly, until thickened and clear. Add lemon juice and butter; stir until melted. Remove from heat and let stand 10 to 15 minutes. Spread over cooled pie. Refrigerate 3 to 4 hours before serving.

PEACHY-YOGURT CHEESECAKE

SERVES 10 TO 12

CRUST
1½ cups graham cracker crumbs
¼ cup sugar
1 teaspoon cinnamon
5 tablespoons butter, melted

FILLING
2 envelopes unflavored gelatin
2 eggs, separated
½ cup milk
½ cup sugar
1 package (8 ounces) cream
    cheese, softened
2 tablespoons lemon juice
1 teaspoon vanilla
1 teaspoon grated lemon peel
2 cups plain yogurt
1 can (16 ounces) sliced peaches,
    drained and finely chopped
½ cup heavy cream

TOPPING
1 cup heavy cream
2 tablespoons confectioners sugar
2 tablespoons sliced blanched
    almonds
Chocolate Caraque or curls
    (optional)

1. **Crust:** Preheat oven to 350°F. Stir graham cracker crumbs, sugar and cinnamon together in small bowl until combined. Pour in melted butter and stir until well blended. Press crumb mixture onto bottom of prepared pan. Bake 10 minutes and cool completely on wire rack.

2. **Filling:** Sprinkle gelatin over ¼ cup cold water, stir to dissolve, and let stand 3 minutes. Place egg yolks, milk and sugar in small saucepan. Cook over low heat, stirring constantly, until sugar is dissolved and mixture is slightly thickened. Stir in gelatin and cook until gelatin is completely dissolved and mixture is thickened; cool.

3. Beat cream cheese until smooth. Add lemon juice, vanilla and lemon peel; beat until well blended. Gradually beat in cooled gelatin mixture. Stir in yogurt, add chopped peaches, and stir to combine. Beat cream until thick and fold in. Beat egg whites until stiff peaks form and fold in. Pour mixture over cooled crust and smooth top. Refrigerate 4 hours, or until set.

4. **Topping:** Beat cream with confectioners sugar until firm. Remove cheesecake from refrigerator and carefully run tip of sharp knife around inside edge of pan. Carefully release side of pan and place cheesecake on serving plate. Spread whipped cream over top, swirling with back of spoon. Sprinkle almonds over whipped cream and arrange Chocolate Caraque or curls on top, if desired.

HINTS AND TIPS

To make Chocolate Caraque, coarsely chop 4 to 6 squares (4 to 6 ounces) semisweet chocolate and place in top of double boiler. Melt chocolate over (not in) simmering water. Remove from heat and pour melted chocolate onto a cold work surface (such as a marble slab) immediately. Spread out the melted chocolate with a long flat icing spatula to about ⅛-inch thickness, making the surface of the chocolate as smooth as possible. Let stand about 3 minutes or until set but not hard. As soon as the chocolate is set, push a metal dough scraper, a wide sharp-edged spatula (paint scraper), or a long sharp knife held lengthwise over the surface of the chocolate. The chocolate will roll up in long thin spirals as you scrape. Lift up the chocolate spirals with a wide spatula and place them on a cold, flat dish or tray. Refrigerate until needed.

To make Chocolate Curls see page 16.

STRAWBERRY MERINGUE BASKET

SERVES 8

MERINGUE
3 egg whites, room temperature
⅛ teaspoon cream of tartar
¾ cup superfine sugar
½ teaspoon vanilla or ¼ teaspoon
 almond extract

FILLING
2 cups heavy cream
1½ teaspoons vanilla
⅓ cup confectioners sugar
1 pint strawberries, hulled, or other
 fresh fruit

1. **Meringue:** Line 2 cookie sheets with parchment paper and draw a 9-inch circle on each sheet. Beat egg whites and cream of tartar together in mixing bowl at high speed until foamy. Gradually sprinkle in sugar, 1 tablespoon at a time, beating constantly. Beat well after each addition, making sure sugar is dissolved before adding the next spoonful. Continue beating at high speed 12 to 15 minutes, or until stiff, glossy peaks form. Beat in vanilla. Rub a little of the beaten meringue between your fingers, and if it feels grainy, continue beating until smooth.

2. Spoon about one-third of beaten whites into large pastry bag fitted with 1-inch star tip. Pipe meringue in a ring around one of the circles; set aside. Spoon remaining meringue into pastry bag and, starting in center of other circle, pipe meringue in a spiral, filling in circle completely.

3. Preheat oven to 275°F. Place cookie sheet with filled-in spiral on top oven rack. Place other cookie sheet on center oven rack. Bake 1½ hours, or until meringues are crisp. Turn off oven and leave meringues in oven 1 hour to dry. Remove from oven and cool completely on cookie sheets. When completely cool, peel off parchment paper. Wrap and store at room temperature until ready to assemble.

4. **Filling:** To assemble the basket, beat cream with vanilla and confectioners sugar until stiff. Place meringue spiral on serving plate. Spoon about ¼ of whipped cream into pastry bag fitted with ½-inch plain tip. Pipe whipped cream on top of outer edge of spiral. Place meringue ring on top to sandwich meringues together. Fill basket with two-thirds of remaining whipped cream and arrange strawberries over top. Pipe remaining whipped cream decoratively around top edge of basket. Serve immediately.

HINTS AND TIPS

Making meringues can be tricky. Let your egg whites come to room temperature before beating—you will get the most volume from warm egg whites. Egg whites should be beaten in a clean bowl with clean beaters. Don't add the sugar all at once; add it gradually, because it must dissolve completely or the baked meringues will be grainy and have small sugar droplets on the outside.

1. Starting in the center of each 4-inch circle, pipe meringue in a spiral until the circle is completely filled.

2. Pipe a ring of meringue around the top edge of each filled circle. Pipe another ring directly on top of the first ring.

3. Bake 50 minutes and let cool in turned-off oven several hours. Fill with sweetened whipped cream or ice cream and top with fresh fruit.

VARIATION

Small Meringue Nests: Prepare meringue mixture as directed above. Spoon meringue into pastry bag fitted with ½-inch plain tip. Draw six 4-inch circles on parchment paper-lined cookie sheets. Starting in center of each circle, pipe meringue in a spiral until circles are completely filled. Change tip on pastry bag to ½-inch star tip and pipe a ring around top edge of each small spiral. Pipe another ring directly on top of first ring. Preheat oven to 275°F. Bake about 50 minutes, or until firm. Turn off oven and leave meringue nests in oven several hours to dry. When completely cool, peel off parchment paper. Fill meringue nests with sweetened whipped cream or ice cream and top with fresh fruit.

CHOCOLATE-HAZELNUT MERINGUE CAKE

SERVES 6 TO 8

MERINGUE
6 egg whites, room temperature
¼ teaspoon cream of tartar
1½ cups superfine sugar
¾ cup very finely chopped or
    ground hazelnuts

FILLINGS
12 ounces sweet chocolate, broken
    into pieces
2 cups heavy cream
1 teaspoon vanilla
¼ cup confectioners sugar

1. Meringue: Preheat oven to 350°F. Line bottoms of three 8-inch round cake pans with parchment paper. Beat egg whites with cream of tartar in large mixing bowl until foamy. Add superfine sugar, 2 tablespoons at a time, beating constantly at high speed until stiff, glossy peaks form.

2. Set aside 2 to 3 tablespoons chopped hazelnuts. Gently fold remaining nuts into beaten whites.

3. Divide egg white mixture evenly among prepared pans and smooth tops. Bake 35 to 40 minutes, or until meringues are crisp on top.

4. Cool in pans on wire racks 1 minute. Carefully invert meringues onto racks, remove pans, and peel off parchment paper. (Meringue bottoms will be soft.) Cool completely on racks.

5. Fillings: Set aside 2 ounces chocolate for decoration and place remaining 10 ounces in heavy saucepan. Add ⅔ cup cream and place over low heat. Cook, stirring constantly, until chocolate is melted and mixture is smooth. Remove from heat and let stand until completely cool, stirring occasionally.

6. Beat remaining 1⅓ cups cream with vanilla and confectioners sugar until firm. Place one meringue on serving plate and spread with one-third of the whipped cream. Pour half of chocolate sauce over top and smooth with small spatula. Top with second meringue. Spread with half of remaining whipped cream. Pour remaining chocolate sauce over top and smooth. Top with third meringue.

7. Pipe or swirl remaining whipped cream around top edge of cake to within ⅛ inch of outside edge. Sprinkle reserved hazelnuts over center of cake. Grate reserved chocolate and sprinkle around top edge of cake, outside whipped cream. Refrigerate 2 to 3 hours. Let stand at room temperature 20 to 30 minutes before serving.

HINTS AND TIPS

To bake the meringues evenly, rotate the cake pans halfway through baking. Unbeaten egg whites can be stored in the refrigerator in a covered container for up to four days, or they may be frozen for up to one year. Defrost and bring to room temperature before beating.

CHOCOLATE BAKED ALASKA

SERVES 8

one 9-inch chocolate layer,
    homemade or prepared from a
    cake mix
2 tablespoons orange juice
2 tablespoons Curacao or orange-
    flavored brandy
1 can (16 ounces) pear slices, well
    drained
1 quart chocolate ice cream
5 egg whites
⅛ teaspoon cream of tartar
½ cup superfine sugar

1. Place cake on freezer-to-oven dish and prick bottom and sides with fork. Combine orange juice and Curacao; sprinkle over cake. Arrange pear slices on top of cake to within ½ inch of edge, placing them as close together as possible.

2. Remove ice cream from container and slice. Place over pears, slicing ice cream to fit. Place in freezer while preparing meringue. (Don't leave cake in freezer too long or fruit will freeze and be too firm to eat.)

3. Preheat oven to 450°F. Beat egg whites with cream of tartar until foamy. Gradually add sugar, 1 tablespoon at a time, beating constantly at high speed until stiff, glossy peaks form.

4. Remove cake from freezer and spread meringue over cake quickly, covering sides and top completely. Swirl meringue into peaks with back of spoon or small, flat spatula. Bake 4 to 6 minutes, or until lightly browned. Serve immediately!

VARIATIONS
Other soft fresh or canned fruit such as well-drained peaches, apricots or pineapple can be substituted for pears. Coffee or French vanilla ice cream can be used instead of chocolate.

HINTS AND TIPS
A Baked Alaska is easy to prepare if you work quickly and follow instructions carefully. To save time, prepare the cake layer ahead of time. Use a 1-layer package of your favorite cake mix. If you don't have a serving dish that can go safely from freezer to oven, place the cake on an aluminum foil-lined cookie sheet. Transfer the finished cake to a serving platter very carefully. Use a large sharp knife to slice the cake.

PIES AND PASTRY

Making a light, flaky pie crust is less complicated than most people think. Follow the simple directions below for a basic pie crust and you will become an expert with very little practice.

MAKES A 9-INCH SINGLE PIE CRUST

1 ¼ cups all-purpose flour
½ teaspoon salt
6 tablespoons chilled shortening *or* 3 tablespoons chilled butter or margarine and 3 tablespoons chilled shortening
3 to 4 tablespoons ice water

FLAKY PASTRY

1. Stir flour and salt together in bowl until well combined. Cut in shortening with pastry blender or 2 knives until mixture is consistency of coarse crumbs. Sprinkle ice water over flour mixture, 1 tablespoon at a time, tossing lightly with fork until mixture is evenly moistened and begins to bind together. Gather dough into ball and flatten slightly with heel of hand. Wrap with plastic wrap or waxed paper and refrigerate 30 minutes.

2. Roll out dough on lightly floured surface to 12-inch circle, rolling dough to about ⅛-inch thickness with lightly floured rolling pin.

3. Carefully wrap dough over rolling pin and unroll over pie plate. Gently ease dough into plate without stretching it. Trim dough to 1 inch beyond rim of plate with sharp knife or scissors. Fold edge under, even with rim of plate, to build up edge, then flute.

4. For prebaked crust, prick bottom and sides of dough. Preheat oven to 425°F. Line dough with aluminum foil and fill with pie weights or dried beans. Bake 8 minutes. Remove aluminum foil and weights, lower oven temperature to 375°F and bake 5 to 7 minutes, or until golden brown. Cool on wire rack.

VARIATION

10-inch single pie crust: Use 1 ½ cups all-purpose flour, ¾ teaspoon salt, 6 tablespoons chilled shortening and 4 to 5 tablespoons ice water. Prepare and bake as directed above.

Clockwise: Amaretti Apricot Tart (page 86), Apple Pastry Strip (page 100), Chocolate-Almond Chiffon Pie (page 92)

Continued

FLUTING THE EDGE

Fork Press edge of pastry flat, even with rim of plate. Dip fork in flour and press prongs of fork firmly around pastry edge.

Crimp Place thumb of one hand against outside edge of rim. Press inside edge of pastry on both sides of thumb with thumb and forefinger of other hand. Repeat around edge.

Scallop Slip tip of knife under edge of pastry and lift pastry slightly. Pinch lifted pastry between your thumb and forefinger. Repeat at 1-inch intervals around pastry edge.

HINTS AND TIPS FOR MAKING PASTRY

● Add ice water to flour 1 tablespoon at a time. Use only enough water to moisten flour until it begins to bind together. If too much water is added, pastry will be tough and may shrink during baking. If not enough water is added, pastry will be crumbly and difficult to roll.

● Avoid stretching pastry to fit pie plate. It will shrink during baking. If pastry tears as it is fitted into pie plate, moisten crack with a little cold water and gently press torn edges together to seal.

● When making pie in unbaked pie shell, don't prick pastry. If you do, the filling will run out through prick holes and cause pastry to stick to pie plate.

DEEP-DISH BLUEBERRY PIE

SERVES 6

PASTRY
¼ cup butter or margarine, softened
1 package (3 ounces) cream cheese, softened
1¼ cups all-purpose flour
2 tablespoons sugar
½ teaspoon salt
2 tablespoons milk or light cream

FILLING
¾ cup sugar
2 tablespoons cornstarch
1 teaspoon grated lemon peel
¼ teaspoon grated nutmeg
6 cups fresh blueberries
1 tablespoon lemon juice
1 tablespoon butter

HINTS AND TIPS
If you don't own a deep pie plate, you can use a 9×2-inch deep cake pan or 2-quart casserole.

1. **Pastry:** Preheat oven to 400°F. Beat butter and cream cheese together in medium-size mixing bowl until well blended. Sift flour, sugar and salt together and stir into creamed mixture, using quick, light strokes. Add milk and stir until dough forms a ball. Wrap with plastic wrap or waxed paper and refrigerate.

2. **Filling:** Combine sugar, cornstarch, lemon peel and nutmeg in large mixing bowl. Add blueberries and toss until well coated. Spoon into deep 9-inch pie plate. Sprinkle with lemon juice and dot with butter.

3. Roll out pastry on lightly floured surface to 12-inch circle. Place pastry over filling. Trim edges to 1 inch beyond rim of pie plate. Fold overhang under and pinch up to form high edge. Flute decoratively. Cut 4 slits in center of pastry to allow steam to escape. Bake 50 to 60 minutes, or until crust is golden brown. Cool completely on wire rack.

VARIATIONS
Blackberry Pie: Use 5 cups hulled blackberries instead of blueberries. Omit lemon juice.
Peach Pie: Use 6 cups peeled, pitted and sliced peaches instead of blueberries. Add ½ teaspoon cinnamon, if desired. Omit lemon peel and increase lemon juice and butter to 2 tablespoons each.

BANANA BLACK-BOTTOM PIE

SERVES 6 TO 8

CRUST
9-inch baked pie crust (page 79)

FILLING
¾ cup sugar
1 tablespoon cornstarch
1 envelope unflavored gelatin
3 eggs, separated
1¼ cups milk
1 teaspoon vanilla
4 squares (4 ounces) unsweetened
  chocolate, melted and cooled
3 bananas
1 tablespoon grated orange peel
2 tablespoons orange-flavored
  brandy
1 teaspoon lemon juice
3 squares (3 ounces) semisweet
  chocolate, coarsely grated

1. **Crust:** Prepare pie crust as directed on page 79. Bake and cool.

2. **Filling:** Stir sugar, cornstarch and gelatin together in heavy saucepan. Beat egg yolks and milk together until well blended. Pour into sugar mixture and stir with wire whisk until mixture is well blended and no lumps remain. Place over low heat and cook, stirring constantly, until mixture is thickened and coats back of spoon. Remove from heat and stir in vanilla. Divide mixture equally between 2 bowls. Stir melted chocolate into 1 bowl until well blended; let cool. Cover other bowl and refrigerate until thickened.

3. Slice 2 bananas and arrange in bottom of cooled pie crust. Pour chocolate mixture over bananas and refrigerate.

4. Stir orange peel and brandy into chilled vanilla custard. Beat egg whites until stiff peaks form and fold in. Pour over chocolate layer in pie and refrigerate 2 to 3 hours, or until set.

5. Remove pie from refrigerator 15 minutes before serving. Cut remaining banana into thick slices and brush slices with lemon juice. Arrange over pie and spoon grated chocolate around banana slices.

HINTS AND TIPS
Bananas, apples and peaches tend to discolor very quickly when peeled and sliced. To prevent this from happening, brush or sprinkle the exposed surface of the fruit immediately with lemon juice or ascorbic acid.

CRANBERRY-APPLE PIE

SERVES 6 TO 8

OLD-FASHIONED PASTRY
2 cups all-purpose flour
1 teaspoon salt
¾ cup chilled shortening or 6
    tablespoons chilled butter or
    margarine and 6 tablespoons
    chilled shortening
1 egg
3 to 4 tablespoons ice water
1 teaspoon cider vinegar

FILLING
1¼ cups sugar
3 tablespoons cornstarch
1 teaspoon cinnamon
½ teaspoon grated nutmeg
2 cups fresh (or frozen and
    thawed) cranberries
3 medium-size apples, peeled,
    cored and chopped
grated peel of 1 orange
milk

1. Old-Fashioned Pastry: Stir flour and salt together in bowl. Cut in shortening with pastry blender or two knives until mixture is consistency of coarse crumbs. Beat egg and 3 tablespoons ice water together with fork until well blended. Beat in vinegar. Sprinkle over flour mixture, 1 tablespoon at a time, tossing lightly with fork until mixture is evenly moistened and begins to bind together. Add remaining 1 tablespoon ice water only if necessary. Gather dough into ball and flatten slightly with heel of hand. Divide dough into two pieces, making one piece slightly larger than the other. Wrap each piece separately with plastic wrap or waxed paper and refrigerate 30 minutes.

2. Roll out larger piece of dough on lightly floured surface to 12-inch circle and use to line 9-inch pie plate. Trim pastry edge to 1 inch beyond rim of plate.

3. Filling: Combine sugar, cornstarch, cinnamon and nutmeg in large mixing bowl. Add cranberries, apples and orange peel; toss until well coated. Spoon into pie crust. Preheat oven to 375°F.

4. Roll out remaining piece of dough to 11-inch circle. Cut dough into ½ - to ¾-inch wide strips with pastry wheel or sharp knife. Brush edge of filled pie crust with water. Arrange half the pastry strips over filling, spacing them about 1¼ inches apart. Press pastry strips at each end to seal. Arrange remaining pastry strips at right angles over other strips to make lattice top. Press ends to seal. Fold edge of bottom crust up and over ends of strips to seal; make a high edge and flute the edge. Brush pastry strips with milk. Cover edge of crust with aluminum foil.

5. Bake 20 minutes. Remove aluminum foil and bake 15 to 20 minutes, or until crust is golden brown and fruit is tender. Cool on wire rack.

HINTS AND TIPS

The addition of vinegar to pie dough makes the dough easy to handle, and produces a very tender and flaky crust. Always flour your rolling pin and work surface before you roll out dough. Use short, quick, light strokes when rolling out dough. Roll from the center of dough to within ½ inch of the edge. Give the dough a quarter turn and roll, repeating the turning and rolling steps until the dough is rolled to the desired size. (Do not roll in several different directions.) If you own a pastry cloth, roll out dough on the cloth. There is no need to flour the surface because pastry cloth is specially treated to prevent dough from sticking. While rolling, flour the rolling pin as little as possible because the addition of too much flour makes pastry tough.

AMARETTI APRICOT TART

SERVES 8 TO 10

PASTRY
1½ cups all-purpose flour
2 tablespoons sugar
¼ teaspoon salt
6 tablespoons butter or margarine
2 egg yolks, beaten

FILLING
½ cup sugar
¼ cup cornstarch
2½ cups milk
4 egg yolks
2 tablespoons butter or margarine
3 tablespoons apricot-flavored
  brandy
1 teaspoon vanilla
1 teaspoon almond extract
½ cup amaretti cookie crumbs

TOPPING
1 can (30 ounces) apricot halves,
  drained
3 tablespoons apricot jam
2 tablespoons apricot-flavored
  brandy (optional)

1. Pastry: Preheat oven to 425°F. Stir flour, sugar and salt together in bowl. Cut in butter until mixture is consistency of coarse crumbs. Add beaten egg yolks and stir until mixture is well combined and binds together. Gather dough and press onto bottom and up sides of 10-inch fluted quiche/flan pan with removable bottom. Prick bottom of crust, line with aluminum foil, and fill with pie weights or dried beans. Bake 8 minutes. Remove aluminum foil and weights, lower oven temperature to 375°F, and bake 8 to 10 minutes. Cool completely on wire rack.

2. Filling: Stir sugar and cornstarch together in heavy saucepan. Add milk and stir with wire whisk until mixture is well blended and no lumps remain. Place over medium heat and cook, stirring constantly, until mixture thickens and comes to a boil. Boil 2 minutes. Remove from heat. Beat egg yolks in small bowl. Stir 4 tablespoons hot milk mixture into beaten yolks, then slowly pour egg yolk mixture back into saucepan, stirring constantly. Return to low heat and cook until thickened; do not let mixture boil. Remove from heat and stir in butter until melted. Press a piece of waxed paper over surface of custard and let stand until cooled. When cool, uncover and stir in 1 tablespoon brandy, vanilla and almond extract.

3. Sprinkle amaretti crumbs with remaining 2 tablespoons brandy and let stand until brandy has been absorbed. Scatter crumbs in bottom of cooled crust. Slowly pour custard filling into crust. Refrigerate until set, about 3 to 4 hours or overnight.

4. Topping: To serve, remove side of pan and slide tart onto serving plate. Place apricot halves, cut side down, on paper towels to drain. Strain apricot jam into small saucepan and place over low heat, stirring until melted. Remove from heat and let cool. Stir in brandy. Arrange apricot halves, cut side down, on top of custard filling. Brush melted jam over apricots to glaze. Serve well chilled.

EGGNOG CHIFFON PIE

SERVES 8 TO 10

PASTRY
1¼ cups all-purpose flour
½ teaspoon salt
6 tablespoons shortening *or* 3
   tablespoons chilled butter or
   margarine and 3 tablespoons
   shortening
3 to 4 tablespoons ice water

FILLING
1 envelope unflavored gelatin
½ cup sugar
⅛ teaspoon salt
1¼ cups milk
3 eggs, separated
2 tablespoons dark rum
1 cup heavy cream
grated nutmeg

1. Pastry: Stir flour and salt together in bowl. Cut in shortening with pastry blender or 2 knives until mixture is consistency of coarse crumbs. Sprinkle ice water over flour mixture, 1 tablespoon at a time, tossing lightly with fork until mixture is evenly moistened and begins to bind together. Gather dough into ball and flatten slightly with heel of hand. Wrap with plastic wrap or waxed paper and refrigerate 30 minutes. Preheat oven to 425°F. Roll out dough on lightly floured surface to 12-inch circle and use to line 9-inch quiche/flan pan with removable bottom. Trim pastry edge even with rim of pan. Lightly prick bottom of pastry with fork. Line with aluminum foil and fill with pie weights or dried beans. Bake 8 minutes. Remove aluminum foil and weights. Lower oven temperature to 375°F and bake 5 to 7 minutes, or until golden brown. Cool completely on wire rack.

2. Filling: Stir gelatin, sugar and salt together in heavy saucepan. Add milk and stir until well blended. Place over low heat and cook, stirring constantly, until gelatin is completely dissolved and mixture is hot. Remove from heat.

3. Beat egg yolks in small bowl. Stir 3 tablespoons hot milk mixture into beaten yolks. Slowly pour egg yolk mixture back into saucepan, stirring constantly. Return to low heat and cook, stirring constantly, until mixture is thickened and coats back of spoon. Remove from heat and let cool. When cool, stir in rum. Pour into large bowl and refrigerate 30 to 45 minutes, or until cold and almost set.

4. Beat cream until firm. Fold whipped cream into chilled custard. Beat egg whites until stiff peaks form. Fold beaten whites into custard. Pour mixture into cooled pie crust. Sprinkle with nutmeg. Refrigerate 4 hours, or until firm.

LEMON MERINGUE PIE

SERVES 6 TO 8

9-inch single pie crust (page 79)

FILLING
½ cup cornstarch
1½ cups granulated sugar
¼ teaspoon salt
2 teaspoons grated lemon peel
½ cup lemon juice
4 egg yolks
1 tablespoon butter or margarine

MERINGUE
4 egg whites
½ cup superfine sugar

1. Prepare and bake pie crust as directed on page 79. Place cornstarch, granulated sugar, salt and lemon peel in heavy saucepan; stir until blended. Add 1¾ cups water and lemon juice slowly. Stir until mixture is well blended and no lumps remain. Cook over medium heat, stirring constantly, until mixture thickens and comes to a boil. Boil 1 minute. Remove from heat.

2. Beat egg yolks in small bowl. Stir in 4 tablespoons hot lemon mixture until blended, then slowly pour egg yolk mixture back into saucepan, stirring constantly. Cook over low heat, stirring constantly, just until thickened; do not allow mixture to boil. Remove from heat and stir in butter until melted. Pour into baked pie crust.

3. Preheat oven to 400°F. Beat egg whites at high speed until soft peaks form. Add superfine sugar, 1 tablespoon at a time, beating constantly at high speed until stiff, glossy peaks form. Spread over filling to edges of pie to seal completely. Swirl meringue with back of spoon. Bake 8 to 10 minutes, or until lightly browned. Cool on wire rack. Chill thoroughly.

NUTTY STREUSEL APPLE PIE

SERVES 8 TO 10

10-inch single pie crust (page 79)

TOPPING
1 cup all-purpose flour
¾ cup firmly packed light brown sugar
½ teaspoon cinnamon
½ cup butter or margarine
½ cup chopped pecans or walnuts

FILLING
3 pounds tart green apples, peeled, cored and sliced (about 10 cups sliced)
1 tablespoon lemon juice
about ½ cup granulated sugar
2 tablespoons cornstarch
2 teaspoons grated lemon peel
1 teaspoon cinnamon
¼ teaspoon grated nutmeg
¼ teaspoon ground cloves

1. Prepare pie crust as directed on page 79 and use to line 10-inch pie plate. Flute edge of pie crust and set aside. Preheat oven to 400°F.

2. **Topping:** Stir flour, brown sugar and cinnamon together in bowl. Cut in butter until mixture is consistency of large crumbs. Stir in nuts until blended; set aside.

3. **Filling:** Place apples in large mixing bowl, sprinkle with lemon juice and toss to coat. Add sugar (adding more sugar if necessary, depending on tartness of apples), cornstarch, lemon peel, cinnamon, nutmeg and cloves. Toss until apples are well coated. Spoon apple mixture into pie crust. Sprinkle topping evenly over apples, covering them completely. Bake 35 to 40 minutes, or until apples are tender and topping is lightly browned. Cool on wire rack. Serve warm or well chilled, topped with sweetened whipped cream or ice cream, if desired.

CHOCOLATE-ALMOND CHIFFON PIE

SERVES 6 TO 8

9-inch baked pie crust (page 79)

FILLING
1 cup milk
½ cup granulated sugar
2 eggs, separated
1 envelope unflavored gelatin
4 squares (4 ounces) semisweet
　chocolate, broken into pieces
grated peel of 1 orange
2 tablespoons dark rum
1 teaspoon vanilla
1 cup heavy cream
2 tablespoons confectioners sugar
½ cup coarsely chopped almonds,
　toasted
grated chocolate (optional)

1. Prepare pie crust as directed on page 79. Bake and cool.

2. **Filling:** Place milk, granulated sugar and egg yolks in heavy saucepan and stir with wire whisk until well blended. Sprinkle gelatin over milk mixture and stir. Add chocolate. Place over low heat and cook, stirring constantly, until chocolate is melted and gelatin is dissolved. Remove from heat, let stand 3 minutes, then stir in orange peel, rum and vanilla. Pour into large mixing bowl and beat at high speed 2 minutes, or until thick and syrupy. Refrigerate 30 to 45 minutes, or until well chilled and almost set.

3. Remove from refrigerator and beat 2 minutes, or until fluffy. Beat cream with confectioners sugar until firm. Reserve 1 cup whipped cream for decoration. Fold remaining whipped cream into chocolate mixture. Beat egg whites until stiff peaks form and fold into chocolate mixture. Scatter almonds in bottom of cooled crust. Pour chocolate mixture into crust. Smooth top and refrigerate 3 hours, or until set.

4. To serve, spoon remaining whipped cream into pastry bag fitted with ½-inch star tip and pipe rosettes around edge of pie. Sprinkle rosettes with grated chocolate, if desired.

HINTS AND TIPS
Caution: Never beat egg whites in an aluminum bowl. The chemical reaction that takes place will cause the egg whites to darken.

PEAR CREME TART

SERVES 6 TO 8

RICH PASTRY
1⅓ cups all-purpose flour
2 tablespoons sugar
¾ teaspoon salt
7 tablespoons sweet butter
1 egg yolk
2 to 3 tablespoons ice water

FILLING
Crème Pâtissière (French Pastry
   Cream), page 97
4 large pears
1½ cups sugar
2 squares (2 ounces) semisweet or
   sweet chocolate, melted

1. **Rich Pastry:** Stir flour, sugar and salt together in bowl until well blended. Cut in butter with pastry blender or 2 knives until mixture is consistency of coarse crumbs. Beat egg yolk with 2 tablespoons ice water and sprinkle over flour mixture, 1 tablespoon at a time, tossing lightly with fork until mixture is evenly moistened and binds together. Add remaining 1 tablespoon ice water only if necessary. Gather dough into a ball and flatten slightly with heel of hand. Wrap with plastic wrap or waxed paper and refrigerate 30 minutes.

2. Preheat oven to 425°F. Roll out dough on lightly floured surface to about ⅛-inch thickness and use to line 9-inch springform pan, pressing dough halfway up sides of pan. Prick the bottom. Line with aluminum foil and fill with pie weights or dried beans. Bake 8 minutes. Remove aluminum foil and weights, lower oven temperature to 375°F, and bake 8 to 10 minutes, or until golden brown. Cool on wire rack.

3. **Filling:** Prepare Crème Pâtissière as directed on page 97. Refrigerate until well chilled, but not set. Peel pears, cut in half lengthwise and remove cores. Place sugar and 1½ cups water in large, heavy saucepan and cook over medium heat 10 minutes, stirring until sugar is dissolved and mixture is syrupy. Add pears to syrup and poach 5 minutes, or until almost tender. Let pears cool in syrup until needed.

4. Spoon Crème Pâtissière into cooled crust and smooth top. Refrigerate, uncovered, about 3 hours, or until set.

5. To serve, carefully release side of pan, slip large, wide spatula under tart, and slide it onto serving plate. Remove pears from syrup and place, cut side down, on paper towels to drain 1 to 2 minutes. Arrange pears, cut side down, on top of Crème Pâtissière. Brush pears with sugar syrup. Drizzle with melted chocolate.

VARIATIONS
Apricot Crème Tart: Use 1 can (17 ounces) apricot halves, well drained. Omit sugar syrup. Melt ⅓ cup strained apricot jam over low heat and cool. Arrange apricots, cut side down, on top of Crème Pâtissière and brush with melted jam. (If fresh apricots are available, use 1 pound fresh apricots and poach in sugar syrup as directed for pears.)
Strawberry Crème Tart: Use 2 pints fresh strawberries, washed and hulled. Melt ½ cup red currant jelly over low heat and cool. Arrange strawberries on top of Crème Pâtissière and brush with melted jelly. Refrigerate 30 minutes before serving.

FRESH FRUIT TARTS

**MAKES 24 SMALL OR
14 LARGE TARTS**

RICH NUT PASTRY
2¼ cups all-purpose flour
¼ cup ground almonds, hazelnuts
   or walnuts
2 tablespoons sugar
1 teaspoon salt
¾ cup chilled sweet butter
2 egg yolks
3 to 4 tablespoons ice water

FILLING
6 fresh apricots or 12 canned
   apricot halves, drained
¼ cup apricot jam
1 pint strawberries
¼ cup red currant jelly

1. Rich Nut Pastry: Stir flour, nuts, sugar and salt together in bowl until well blended. Cut in butter with pastry blender or 2 knives until mixture is consistency of coarse crumbs. Blend egg yolks with 3 tablespoons ice water until smooth. Sprinkle egg yolk mixture over flour mixture, 1 tablespoon at a time, tossing lightly with fork until mixture is evenly moistened and begins to bind together. Add remaining 1 tablespoon ice water only if necessary. Gather dough into a ball and flatten slightly with heel of hand. Divide dough into 2 equal pieces. Wrap each piece separately with plastic wrap or waxed paper and refrigerate 30 minutes.

2. Preheat oven to 425°F. Roll out dough, half at a time, on a lightly floured surface to about ⅛- to ¼-inch thickness. Cut into rounds with floured 3-inch fluted cutter. Roll out remaining piece of pastry and cut in the same manner. Gather trimmings, reroll, and cut into rounds, making as many additional tarts as needed. Place 1 dough circle in each mold of two 12-cup tart pans, pressing dough well into sides of each mold. Cut twenty-four 3-inch circles of aluminum foil and use to line each pastry shell. Fill with pie weights or dried beans and bake 8 minutes. Remove aluminum foil and weights, lower oven temperature to 375°F and bake 5 minutes, or until golden. Cool in pans on wire racks. Remove pastry from pans.

3. Filling: Peel and pit apricots. Place 1 apricot half, cut side down, into each of 12 cooled pastry shells. Strain apricot jam into small saucepan and heat until melted. Brush over each apricot half.

4. Wash, drain and hull strawberries. Place 3 to 4 small strawberries into each of the remaining 12 pastry shells. If strawberries are large, cut into thick slices and arrange slices in pastry shells. Melt red currant jelly in small saucepan and brush over strawberries. Let stand until glaze is set.

VARIATION
Large tarts: Use 3½-inch deep fluted tart pans to make 14 large tarts. Fill half the tarts with apricots and the remainder with strawberries.

Picture, see page 95

CREAM PUFFS

MAKES 12

CHOUX PASTE
½ cup sweet butter
1 cup water
1 tablespoon sugar
¼ teaspoon salt
1 cup all-purpose flour
4 eggs

FLAVORED WHIPPED CREAM:
(enough to fill 12 Cream Puffs, 24
Profiteroles (Miniature Cream Puffs), 16
Eclairs or 1 Cream Puff Ring (Paris-Brest))
2 cups heavy cream
1½ teaspoons almond extract or
   2 teaspoons vanilla
⅓ cup confectioners sugar

CRÈME PÂTISSIÈRE:
(French Pastry Cream—enough to fill
12 Cream Puffs, 24 Profiteroles, 16 Eclairs
or 1 Cream Puff Ring (Paris-Brest))
¼ cup all-purpose flour
2 tablespoons cornstarch
½ cup granulated sugar
¼ teaspoon salt
2 cups milk
6 egg yolks, lightly beaten
2 teaspoons vanilla
1 cup heavy cream
2 tablespoons confectioners sugar

1. Choux Paste: Grease 2 cookie sheets. Place butter, water, sugar and salt in heavy saucepan and bring to a full rolling boil. Remove from heat and add flour, all at once, stirring vigorously with wooden spoon until mixture comes away from side of pan and forms a ball. Let stand 5 minutes.

2. Add eggs, 1 at a time, beating well after each addition and making sure that each egg is thoroughly combined before adding next.

3. Preheat oven to 375°F. Drop mixture by heaping spoonfuls into 12 large mounds onto prepared cookie sheets, spacing them about 3 inches apart. Swirl top of each mound. Bake 45 minutes. Remove from oven and cut a slit in side of each puff. Return to oven and bake 10 minutes, or until golden brown. Remove from cookie sheets and cool on wire racks. Prepare desired filling.

4. Flavored Whipped Cream: Beat cream and almond extract together until thick. Gradually beat in ⅓ cup confectioners sugar, beating until stiff. Use to fill pastry.

Crème Pâtissière (French Pastry Cream): Combine flour, cornstarch, granulated sugar and salt in heavy saucepan. Stir in milk with wire whisk until mixture is well blended and no lumps remain. Place over low heat and cook, stirring constantly, until mixture thickens and comes to a boil. Boil gently 1 minute. Remove from heat. Stir 3 tablespoons hot milk mixture into beaten yolks, then slowly pour egg yolk mixture into the saucepan, stirring constantly. Return to low heat and cook, stirring constantly, until mixture is thickened and coats back of spoon; do not let mixture boil. Remove from heat and stir 2 minutes to cool. Stir in vanilla. Pour custard into bowl and cover surface with waxed paper (to prevent skin from forming). Refrigerate 3 hours, or until well chilled. Beat cream with confectioners sugar until stiff. Remove custard from refrigerator and fold in whipped cream. Use to fill pastry.

5. Cut tops off each puff and scoop out any soft dough. Spoon desired filling into shells and replace tops. Sprinkle with confectioners sugar. Refrigerate until ready to serve.

VARIATIONS

Eclairs: Prepare choux paste as directed above. Spoon mixture into large pastry bag fitted with ½-inch plain tip. Pipe eclairs about 4 inches long and 1 inch wide onto greased cookie sheets, spacing them 2 inches apart. Preheat oven to 375°F. Bake 30 minutes. Remove from oven and cut a slit about 2 inches long in side of each
Continued

eclair. Return to oven and bake 10 minutes, or until golden brown. Cool on wire racks. To fill, cut eclairs in half lengthwise and remove any soft dough. Spread or pipe desired filling onto bottom halves of eclairs and replace tops. Frost with Bittersweet Chocolate Glaze (below), if desired. Makes 16 eclairs.

Profiteroles (Miniature Cream Puffs): Prepare choux paste as directed above. Drop mixture by heaping teaspoonfuls into 24 mounds onto greased cookie sheets, spacing them about 2 inches apart. Swirl top of each mound. Preheat oven to 375°F. Bake 20 minutes. Remove from oven and cut a slit in side of each puff. Return to oven and bake 10 minutes, or until golden brown. Cool on wire racks. Fill with desired filling as directed for Cream Puffs. Arrange filled puffs on serving plate and top with Rich Chocolate Sauce (below), if desired.

Cream Puff Ring (Paris-Brest): Prepare choux paste as directed above. Draw 8-inch circle on parchment paper-lined cookie sheet. Spoon choux mixture into large pastry bag fitted with 1-inch plain tip. Pipe mixture in a ring following circle on parchment paper. Or, drop mixture by heaping spoonfuls inside circle to make a ring. Preheat oven to 400°F. Bake 35 to 40 minutes, or until golden brown. Cool on wire rack. Cut choux ring in half horizontally with sharp knife. Remove soft dough from inside to make a hollow shell. Fill with Crème Pâtissière (above) and replace top. Top with Bittersweet Chocolate Glaze (below) and refrigerate until ready to serve.

MAKES 1 CUP

2 squares (2 ounces) unsweetened chocolate, broken into small pieces
2 tablespoons sweet butter
1 tablespoon light corn syrup
1 cup confectioners sugar
1 tablespoon plus 1 teaspoon milk or light cream

BITTERSWEET CHOCOLATE GLAZE

Place chocolate, butter and corn syrup in heavy saucepan over low heat. Cook, stirring constantly, until chocolate is melted. Remove from heat, add confectioners sugar and milk, and stir until smooth and glossy. Spread over tops of filled eclairs or Cream Puff Ring.

MAKES 1¼ CUPS

6 squares (6 ounces) semisweet chocolate, broken into small pieces or 1 cup semisweet chocolate morsels
2 tablespoons sweet butter
⅓ cup light corn syrup
¼ cup light cream or milk
1 teaspoon vanilla
1 to 2 teaspoons instant coffee powder (optional)

RICH CHOCOLATE SAUCE

Place chocolate, butter and corn syrup in heavy saucepan over low heat. Cook, stirring constantly, until chocolate is melted. Remove from heat and stir in cream, vanilla and coffee until smooth. (If sauce seems too thick, stir in 1 to 2 tablespoons additional cream.) Spoon over filled Profiteroles.

APPLE PASTRY STRIP

SERVES 6

1 package (17¼ ounces) frozen
   puff pastry, thawed

FILLING
1 cup prepared mincemeat
1 large tart apple
1 egg, beaten
confectioners sugar

1. Unfold sheets of puff pastry and lay flat on lightly-floured surface. Fold 1 sheet of pastry in half lengthwise and roll out to 6 × 12-inch rectangle, about ¼- to ½-inch thick. Place pastry rectangle on ungreased cookie sheet.

2. **Filling:** Spread mincemeat over rectangle to within 1 inch of edges. Peel, core and thinly slice apple. Arrange apple slices on top of mincemeat in overlapping rows. Trim pastry edges to make a neat rectangle and brush edges with some of beaten egg.

3. Fold second sheet of pastry in half lengthwise and roll out to same size as first; fold in half lengthwise again. Cut slits in folded pastry, about ¼ inch apart, through folded edge to within 1 inch of outside edge; make sure slits go through folded pastry. Unfold the pastry and carefully place it on top of filling. Press edges of pastry together all around rectangle to seal. Place blunt edge of floured knife horizontally against pastry edge and gently tap knife around edges, making several cuts in pastry each place you tap. To flute edges, place a fingertip on rim of pastry and, holding floured knife pointed down, draw knife up against the pastry edge. Use quick, slanting strokes. Repeat at ¼-inch intervals all around pastry edge.

4. Preheat oven to 425°F. Brush pastry all over with remaining beaten egg. Bake 10 minutes. Lower oven temperature to 375°F and bake 10 minutes, or until golden. Remove from oven and sprinkle with sifted confectioners sugar. Bake 8 to 10 minutes, or until crisp and golden brown. Cool on cookie sheet 5 minutes.

5. Slide large, wide spatula under pastry strip and carefully slide pastry onto serving plate. Sprinkle with additional confectioners sugar and serve warm with sweetened whipped cream, if desired.

RASPBERRY NAPOLEON

SERVES 6

1 sheet frozen puff pastry (½ of
    17¼-ounce package), thawed

FILLING
1 cup heavy cream
2 tablespoons confectioners sugar
1 teaspoon vanilla
sugar
⅓ cup raspberry jam

CONFECTIONERS ICING
1 cup confectioners sugar, sifted
1 tablespoon corn syrup
red food coloring

1. Unfold pastry and lay flat on lightly floured surface. Roll out to 12 × 16-inch rectangle. Cut lengthwise into 3 equal strips. Place strips on ungreased cookie sheet, spacing them about 2 inches apart. Prick each strip all over with fork. Place in refrigerator 10 to 15 minutes.

2. Preheat oven to 425°F. Remove from refrigerator and bake 8 to 10 minutes, or until pastry is golden and well risen. Turn strips over and bake 3 to 4 minutes. Remove from oven and cool completely on wire rack.

3. **Filling:** Beat cream until thick. Add confectioners sugar and vanilla; continue beating until firm.

4. To assemble, place pastry strips on work surface and trim edges of each strip with sharp knife. Spread 1 pastry strip with half the jam. Spread half the whipped cream over jam. Place on long, flat serving plate. Spread second pastry strip with remaining jam and whipped cream. Carefully position on top of first pastry strip. Remove any whipped cream that drips over edges with small spatula.

5. **Confectioners Icing:** Place confectioners sugar in top of double boiler over simmering water. Add corn syrup and 1 tablespoon water and heat, stirring constantly, until sugar is dissolved and mixture is smooth. (Icing should be soft and thick enough to coat back of spoon.) Place remaining pastry strip on wire rack set over a piece of waxed paper. Spoon some of the icing over top of pastry strip and spread with small icing spatula, completely covering top. Thin remaining icing with a little water and stir in a few drops of red food coloring to tint. Spoon pink icing into small pastry bag fitted with small plain writing tip. Pipe pink icing across top of pastry strip in parallel lines about ½ to ¾ inch apart. Draw metal skewer or point of sharp knife across piped lines in alternate directions. Let icing set. Carefully place iced pastry strip on top of other strips.

6. Refrigerate 30 minutes before serving. Cut with very sharp knife.

BANANA SPICE ENVELOPES

MAKES 16

1 package (17¼ ounces) frozen
   puff pastry, thawed

FILLING
4 large firm bananas
1 to 2 tablespoons lemon juice
½ cup granulated sugar
1 teaspoon pumpkin pie spice or
   ½ teaspoon cinnamon,
   ¼ teaspoon grated nutmeg and
   ¼ teaspoon ground cloves
1 egg, beaten with 1 tablespoon
   water
confectioners sugar

1. Preheat oven to 425°F. Unfold sheets of puff pastry and lay flat on lightly floured surface. Roll out pastry, 1 sheet at a time, to two 10 × 20-inch rectangles. Trim edges with sharp knife to even. Cut each rectangle into eight 5-inch squares.

2. **Filling:** Cut bananas crosswise into 4 equal-size pieces. Brush each piece with lemon juice to prevent discoloring. Mix granulated sugar and pumpkin pie spice in small bowl. Roll each piece of banana in sugar-spice mixture to coat. Place coated banana piece diagonally in center of pastry square. Repeat with remaining banana pieces and pastry squares. Brush edges of pastry squares with some of the beaten egg mixture.

3. Bring opposite corners of pastry into center, 1 corner slightly overlapping the other. Bring other 2 corners into the center, corners overlapping (banana will be completely enclosed). Press down firmly in center to seal corners. Fold edges of pastry over each other slightly and press to seal.

4. Brush pastry with remaining beaten egg mixture and sprinkle with remaining sugar-spice mixture. Place envelopes on ungreased cookie sheets, spacing them about 1 to 2 inches apart. Bake 10 minutes. Lower oven temperature to 350°F and bake 8 to 10 minutes, or until pastry is puffed and golden brown.

5. Remove envelopes from cookie sheets with wide spatula and cool on wire racks. Sprinkle with confectioners sugar just before serving.

HINTS AND TIPS

Don't stretch pastry while rolling it out. Stretching will cause pastry to shrink during baking.

After the pastry has been rolled out, let it rest 5 to 10 minutes before cutting into squares.

APPLE STRUDEL

SERVES 8 TO 10

¾ cup butter
2 cups fresh white bread crumbs
½ pound filo/strudel leaves (about 8 to 10 leaves), thawed if frozen
6 medium-size tart apples (about 2 pounds), peeled, cored and thinly sliced
½ cup granulated sugar
½ teaspoon cinnamon
¼ teaspoon ground cloves
¼ teaspoon grated nutmeg
grated peel of 1 lemon
½ cup raisins
½ cup chopped almonds, hazelnuts or walnuts
confectioners sugar

1. Preheat oven to 375°F. Grease 10 × 15-inch jelly-roll pan or large cookie sheet.

2. Melt ¼ cup butter in heavy skillet. Stir in bread crumbs and cook until brown and crisp. Remove from heat; set aside. Melt remaining ½ cup butter in small saucepan.

3. Unfold strudel leaves and place on large sheet of waxed paper. Cover with clean, damp dish towel. Remove 1 strudel leaf, place on damp dish towel, and brush with some of the melted butter. Place second leaf on top of first, and brush with some of the melted butter, keeping remaining leaves covered while you work. Continue in same manner with remaining leaves. Sprinkle all but ⅓ cup browned bread crumbs over top leaf.

4. Arrange apple slices on top leaf in a row about 3 inches in from 1 long edge. Combine granulated sugar, cinnamon, cloves, nutmeg, lemon peel, raisins, nuts and remaining ⅓ cup bread crumbs; spoon over apple slices.

5. Fold long edge of pastry closest to apples over filling. With aid of towel, gradually roll up strudel, jelly-roll fashion, patting roll to keep shape even. Brush seam with water and press gently to seal. Tuck in ends. Lift strudel in towel and roll onto prepared pan, seam side down. Brush generously with remaining melted butter.

6. Bake 35 to 40 minutes, or until just golden brown. Remove from oven and let cool in pan on wire rack 30 minutes. Dust with confectioners sugar just before serving and cut into thick slices. Serve warm or at room temperature, topped with sweetened whipped cream or ice cream, if desired.

HINTS AND TIPS
The flavor of strudel is best when it is served warm. Reheat in low oven 10 to 15 minutes just before serving.

1. Sprinkle browned bread crumbs evenly over pastry.

2. Arrange apple slices over strudel leaves in a row about 3 inches in from long edge.

3. Spoon combined sugar, cinnamon, cloves, nutmeg, lemon peel, raisins, nuts and bread crumbs over apple slices.

4. Fold long edge of pastry closest to apples over filling. With aid of towel, gradually roll up the strudel, jelly-roll fashion, patting roll to keep shape even.

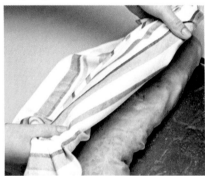

5. Brush seam with water and press gently to seal. Tuck in ends. Lift strudel in towel and roll onto prepared pan.

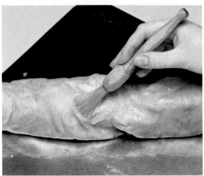

6. Brush the strudel generously with remaining melted butter. Bake 35 to 40 minutes, or until just golden brown.

COOKIES

It is a tossup which, in the long run, is more fun—baking cookies or eating them. There are few things easier to bake than cookies, and if there are children around, cookie baking can provide some wonderful shared activity on a rainy day.

Cookies generally fall into one of five categories. The category is determined by the shape of the cookie:

Drop: The dough is dropped from a spoon onto a cookie sheet.

Rolled: The dough is rolled out on a lightly floured surface and cut into shapes with a sharp knife or a cookie cutter.

Molded: The dough is shaped by hand, squeezed through a pastry bag, or pressed through a cookie press.

Refrigerator: The dough is shaped into a roll, wrapped and chilled in the refrigerator, and sliced before baking.

Bar: The dough is baked in a square or rectangular pan and then cut into bars or squares.

HINTS AND TIPS FOR MAKING COOKIES

● Weather can affect certain kinds of cookies. Cookies that are supposed to become firm and crisp while cooling should not be baked on a day when the humidity is high.

● Bring all ingredients to room temperature before mixing.

● Preheat oven and place filled cookie sheet in the center of the oven, leaving space on all sides for air to circulate.

● Follow recipe instructions carefully in regard to whether or not the cookie sheet should be greased. Some cookies will spread too much if baked on a greased cookie sheet. On the other hand, there are some cookies that will stick to the cookie sheet if it is not greased.

● Always place cookies well apart on the cookie sheet to allow room for expansion.

● If you are not in a hurry, it is best to bake 1 cookie sheet at a time. If you have more than 1 cookie sheet in the oven, or if your oven bakes unevenly, rotate cookie sheet(s) halfway through baking.

● Most cookies bake very quickly. Use a timer so you can check cookies after the minimum baking time. If some cookies are done ahead of the others, remove them to a wire rack to cool while the remainder finish baking.

● It is easier to remove baked cookies from a cookie sheet that does not have sides, than from a pan with sides, such as a jelly-roll pan. If you own only 1 cookie sheet and want to prepare a second batch of cookies to go in the oven, turn a jelly-roll pan or rectangular metal baking dish upside-down and place the cookies on the bottom of the pan.

● When making cookies in batches, allow the cookie sheet to cool between batches. Wipe off any crumbs from first batch that might burn.

Clockwise: Rich Pecan Bars (page 110), Almond Tuiles (page 122), Macadamia Chip Cookies (page 110)

MACADAMIA CHIP COOKIES

MAKES ABOUT 4 DOZEN

½ cup butter or margarine,
  softened
½ cup granulated sugar
½ cup firmly packed light brown
  sugar
1 egg
1 teaspoon vanilla
1 cup plus 2 tablespoons
  all-purpose flour
½ teaspoon salt
¼ teaspoon baking soda
½ cup chopped macadamia nuts
½ cup mini semisweet chocolate
  chips

1. Preheat oven to 375°F. Lightly grease 2 large cookie sheets.

2. Beat butter and sugars together in medium-size mixing bowl until light and fluffy. Beat in egg and vanilla until well blended.

3. Sift flour, salt and baking soda together. Gradually beat flour mixture into creamed mixture until thoroughly combined. Stir in nuts and chocolate until blended.

4. Drop mixture by teaspoonfuls onto prepared cookie sheets, spacing cookies about 2 inches apart. Bake 6 to 8 minutes, or until edges of cookies are golden brown.

5. Remove from cookie sheets with wide spatula and place on wire racks to cool and harden.

Picture, see page 108

RICH PECAN BARS

MAKES ABOUT 3 DOZEN

BARS
1½ cups all-purpose flour
1 teaspoon cinnamon
¼ teaspoon baking soda
½ cup butter or margarine
¾ cup sugar
1 egg
1 tablespoon strong black coffee

PECAN TOPPING
3 egg whites
½ teaspoon cinnamon
½ cup confectioners sugar
2 cups chopped pecans

1. **Bars:** Preheat oven to 350°F. Sift flour, cinnamon and baking soda together; set aside. Beat butter in mixing bowl until creamy. Beat in sugar until light and fluffy. Add egg and coffee; beat until well blended. Gradually add flour mixture, beating constantly, until thoroughly blended.

2. Spread dough evenly onto bottom of ungreased 9 × 13-inch baking pan. Press dough well into corners of pan with fingertips. Bake 20 minutes.

3. **Pecan Topping:** Beat egg whites until foamy. Add cinnamon and confectioners sugar; beat just until soft peaks form. Fold in pecans. Remove crust from oven and spread Pecan Topping evenly over crust, pressing down lightly with flat bladed knife.

4. Return to oven and bake 15 to 20 minutes, or until topping is lightly browned. Cool in pan on wire rack. Score into 36 bars while warm. When cold, cut into bars and remove from pan.

Picture, see page 108

PEANUT COOKIES

MAKES ABOUT 3 DOZEN

1½ cups all-purpose flour
½ teaspoon baking soda
6 tablespoons butter or margarine,
   softened
¾ cup firmly packed light brown
   sugar
1 egg
¾ cup ground or finely chopped
   salted peanuts
salted peanut halves

1. Preheat oven to 375°F. Lightly grease 2 cookie sheets.

2. Stir flour and baking soda together; set aside.

3. Beat butter until very creamy. Beat in brown sugar until light and fluffy. Add egg and beat until thoroughly blended. Stir in flour mixture and ground peanuts until thoroughly combined; dough will be stiff.

4. Measure teaspoonfuls of dough and shape into small balls. Place balls on prepared cookie sheets, spacing them about 1½ inches apart. Flatten with back of spoon. Press 1 peanut half into center of each cookie.

5. Bake 8 to 10 minutes, or until edges of cookies are just firm to the touch.

6. Remove from cookie sheets with spatula and cool on wire racks.

HINTS AND TIPS
To grind peanuts in a food processor, place about 1 cup peanuts in bowl of food processor. Process with the metal blade, using the quick "on–off" technique (or use the pulse button if your machine has one). Keep a careful eye on the peanuts; total processing time should be about 30 seconds. If you do not check the peanuts every 5 to 10 seconds, you will have peanut butter instead of ground nuts.

FROSTED FUDGIE BROWNIES

MAKES 1 DOZEN

BROWNIES
1 cup all-purpose flour
½ teaspoon baking powder
¼ teaspoon salt
½ cup butter or margarine
2 squares (2 ounces) unsweetened
  chocolate
1 cup sugar
2 eggs
1 teaspoon vanilla
½ cup chopped walnuts, pecans or
  almonds (optional)

FUDGIE FROSTING
2 tablespoons butter
1 square (1 ounce) unsweetened
  chocolate
1 cup confectioners sugar
1½ tablespoons milk

1. **Brownies:** Preheat oven to 350°F. Grease 7 × 11-inch or 9-inch square baking pan.

2. Sift flour, baking powder and salt together; set aside.

3. Melt butter and chocolate together in saucepan over low heat. Remove from heat and stir in sugar. Let cool. Add eggs and vanilla; stir until well blended. Thoroughly fold in flour mixture. Stir in nuts. Spread mixture in prepared pan.

4. Bake 25 minutes.

5. Remove from oven and cool completely in pan on wire rack.

6. **Frosting:** Melt butter and chocolate together in saucepan over low heat. Remove from heat and stir in confectioners sugar and milk until smooth. (If mixture seems too thick to spread, add 1 to 2 teaspoons additional milk.) Spread frosting over brownies, using flat-bladed knife; let stand 15 to 20 minutes, or until frosting is set. When set, cut brownies into squares and remove from pan.

VARIATIONS

Butterscotch Brownies: Prepare as directed above, omitting chocolate. Use dark brown sugar instead of granulated sugar and stir in 1 tablespoon molasses along with brown sugar, if desired. Increase chopped nuts to ¾ cup and stir in ½ cup butterscotch-flavored morsels. Bake 30 minutes. Frost if desired.

Choco-Chip Brownies: Prepare as directed for Frosted Fudgey Brownies, using dark brown sugar instead of granulated sugar. Stir in ¾ cup semisweet chocolate pieces. Bake 25 minutes. Frost if desired.

HINTS AND TIPS
It is important to preheat the oven to the correct temperature. Take care not to overbake brownies—the longer they bake, the harder and less fudgie they will be.

CHOCOLATE NUGGETS

MAKES ABOUT 3½ DOZEN

1 cup all-purpose flour
½ teaspoon baking soda
¼ teaspoon salt
½ cup butter or margarine
½ cup firmly packed dark brown
  sugar
¼ cup granulated sugar
1 egg, beaten
1 teaspoon vanilla
1 cup mini semisweet chocolate
  chips or 6 squares (6 ounces)
  semisweet chocolate, chopped
½ cup chopped walnuts, pecans or
  almonds

1. Preheat oven to 375°F.

2. Sift flour, baking soda and salt together; set aside.

3. Cream butter and sugars together in large mixing bowl until light and fluffy. Beat in egg and vanilla. Gradually add flour mixture, beating until well blended and smooth. Stir in chocolate and nuts.

4. Drop mixture by well-rounded teaspoonfuls onto ungreased cookie sheets, spacing them about 2 inches apart.

5. Bake 10 minutes, or until edges of cookies are firm to the touch.

6. Remove from cookie sheets with spatula and place on wire racks to cool and harden.

HINTS AND TIPS

If using more than 1 cookie sheet in the oven at a time, rotate the cookie sheets halfway through baking, reversing the top and bottom sheets so the cookies bake evenly. Be sure your cookie sheets do not touch the oven walls and that they are not placed directly over each other. Stagger them in the oven so air can circulate around them.

CHINESE ALMOND CAKES

MAKES 1½ DOZEN

1½ cups all-purpose flour
½ teaspoon baking powder
¼ teaspoon salt
½ cup butter or margarine
¾ cup sugar
1 egg
1 teaspoon almond extract
blanched whole almonds
1 egg, beaten

1. Sift flour, baking powder and salt together; set aside.

2. Cream butter and sugar together until light and fluffy. Beat in egg and almond extract. Stir in flour mixture until well combined.

3. Place dough on well floured surface, knead 5 to 6 strokes or until smooth. Shape into flattened round. Wrap dough with waxed paper and refrigerate 30 minutes.

4. Preheat oven to 350°F. Lightly grease 2 cookie sheets.

5. Remove dough from refrigerator, unwrap and divide in half. Cut each half into 9 equal-size pieces. Shape each piece into a ball. Place balls on prepared cookie sheets and flatten with heel of hand or bottom of glass. Press an almond in center of each cake. Brush with beaten egg.

6. Bake about 15 minutes, or until golden.

7. Remove from cookie sheets with spatula and cool on wire racks.

GINGER-CREAM SANDWICH COOKIES

MAKES ABOUT 1½ DOZEN

COOKIES
3 cups all-purpose flour
½ teaspoon baking soda
¼ teaspoon salt
1½ teaspoons ground ginger
¼ teaspoon ground cloves
½ cup butter or margarine, softened
½ cup firmly packed light brown sugar
⅓ cup molasses
2 tablespoons honey
1 egg

CREAM FILLING
2 tablespoons butter or margarine
1½ cups confectioners sugar, sifted
¼ teaspoon ground ginger
1 to 2 tablespoons boiling water

1. Cookies: Sift flour, baking soda, salt, ginger and cloves together; set aside. Cream butter and brown sugar in large mixing bowl until light and fluffy. Beat in molasses, honey and egg until well blended. Gradually beat in flour mixture, beating well after each addition, until smooth. Shape dough into ball. Wrap with waxed paper and refrigerate 30 minutes.

2. Preheat oven to 350°F. Grease 2 cookie sheets. Remove dough from refrigerator and roll out, half the dough at a time, as thinly as possible (no more than ⅛ inch thick) on lightly floured surface. Cut dough into rounds with plain 2½-inch round cookie cutter. Place rounds on prepared cookie sheets, spacing them about 1 inch apart. Bake 10 to 12 minutes, or until just firm to the touch. Remove from cookie sheets and cool on wire racks.

3. Cream Filling: Beat butter, confectioners sugar and ginger in small bowl until light. Beat in enough boiling water to make mixture smooth and good spreading consistency. Spread Cream Filling over bottom side of half the cookies and top with remaining cookies, bottom side down. Lightly press cookies together.

GINGERBREAD MEN

MAKES ABOUT 2 DOZEN

2 ½ cups flour
1 ½ teaspoons ground ginger
1 teaspoon cinnamon
½ teaspoon baking soda
½ teaspoon salt
½ teaspoon ground allspice
¼ teaspoon ground cloves
½ cup butter or margarine,
  softened
½ cup sugar
½ cup molasses
1 egg
currants
thinly sliced candied cherries

1. Sift flour, ginger, cinnamon, baking soda, salt, allspice and cloves together; set aside. Cream butter and sugar in large mixing bowl until light and fluffy. Add molasses and egg; beat until well blended. Gradually beat in flour mixture, beating at medium speed, until well combined.

2. Cover and refrigerate 2 to 3 hours or overnight.

3. Preheat oven to 350°F. Grease 2 large cookie sheets. Remove dough from refrigerator and roll out to ⅛-inch thickness on lightly floured surface. Cut dough with floured 5-inch gingerbread cookie cutter. Carefully lift cookies with wide spatula and place on prepared cookie sheets, spacing them about 1 inch apart. Gather trimmings, reroll, and cut more cookies.

4. Press currants into cookies to make eyes and buttons. Use thin slice of candied cherry to make mouth. Bake 8 to 10 minutes, or until lightly browned. Remove from cookie sheets with wide spatula and cool on wire racks.

HINTS AND TIPS

These cookies keep very well stored in an airtight container. Make them ahead for the holidays and freeze flat in a single layer. When frozen, transfer to a freezer container or plastic freezer bag, seal, label and date. Thaw, wrapped, at room temperature.

TIGER COOKIES

MAKES ABOUT 1½ DOZEN

COOKIES
¾ cup butter or margarine
1 cup sugar
1 egg, beaten
1 teaspoon vanilla
2 cups all-purpose flour
½ teaspoon baking powder
¼ teaspoon salt

FROSTING AND DECORATION
2 teaspooons instant coffee
   powder
about 1 tablespoon warm milk or
   light cream
4 tablespoons butter or margarine
1½ cups confectioners sugar
chocolate sprinkles
sifted confectioners sugar

1. Cookies: Cream butter and sugar together in mixing bowl until light and fluffy. Beat in egg and vanilla until well blended. Stir flour, baking powder and salt together and add to creamed mixture, stirring with wooden spoon until well combined. Shape dough on waxed paper, making 2 logs, each about 6 inches long and 2 inches wide. Wrap each log with waxed paper or plastic wrap and refrigerate about 3 hours, or until firm.

2. Preheat oven to 375°F. Grease 2 cookie sheets. Remove dough from refrigerator and unwrap. Cut each log into ⅛-inch thick slices. Place slices on prepared cookie sheets, spacing them 1½ inches apart. Bake 10 to 12 minutes, or until just golden.

3. Cool on cookie sheets 1 minute, then remove from cookie sheets and cool completely on wire racks.

4. Frosting and Decoration: Dissolve coffee in warm milk. Beat butter, confectioners sugar and coffee mixture together until well blended, adding more milk if necessary, and beating until frosting is smooth and good spreading consistency. Spread bottoms of half the cookies with frosting and top with remaining cookies, bottom side down. Spread a little frosting around sides of each filled cookie. Place chocolate sprinkles on plate and roll cookies in sprinkles to coat edges. Sprinkle confectioners sugar over tops, if desired.

ALMOND TUILES

MAKES ABOUT 3 DOZEN

2 egg whites
½ cup sugar
½ teaspoon vanilla
¼ teaspoon almond extract
⅓ cup all-purpose flour, sifted
¼ cup finely ground almonds
¼ cup butter, melted and cooled
½ cup sliced or slivered almonds

1. Preheat oven to 425°F. Grease and flour 2 large cookie sheets. Beat egg whites in medium-size mixing bowl until foamy. Add sugar and continue beating until stiff peaks form. Beat in vanilla and almond extract. Sprinkle flour and ground almonds over beaten whites and gently but thoroughly fold in until well blended. Gradually fold in melted butter.

2. Drop mixture by teaspoonfuls onto prepared cookie sheets, spacing them about 3 to 4 inches apart. Spread each mound as thinly and evenly as possible with small, flat spatula or knife. Sprinkle each cookie with sliced almonds.

3. Bake in upper third of the oven 5 to 7 minutes, or until edges of cookies are golden brown.

4. Remove from oven. Remove each cookie from cookie sheet promptly with wide spatula and press it around rolling pin or drinking glass, almond side out. Leave cookies on rolling pin 1 to 2 minutes, then carefully remove to wire rack to cool and crisp. Bake and shape remaining cookies in same manner.

VARIATIONS

Large Tuiles: Drop mixture by tablespoonfuls onto prepared cookie sheets, spreading them as directed above.
Rolled Cigarettes: Prepare as directed above, omitting sliced almonds. Bake as directed above. Roll each cookie around handle of wooden spoon or pencil. Leave cookies on spoon handle 1 to 2 minutes. Carefully slip cookies off spoon handle onto wire racks to cool and crisp.

HINTS AND TIPS

It may be necessary to turn the cookie sheet during baking so cookies will brown evenly. Bake 1 cookie sheet at a time until you become adept at baking and shaping these cookies. You will only be able to make about 4 to 5 cookies at one time. Working quickly is very important. Do not allow the cookies to remain on the cookie sheet because they will become brittle and impossible to roll and shape. In order to be rolled properly, these cookies must be soft and pliable. If the cookies harden before you can roll them, return them to the oven for 1 to 2 minutes to soften. These cookies do not keep well and should be stored in an airtight container as soon as they are cool. They can also be frozen until needed. If frozen, thaw, covered, at room temperature.

ALMOND-BUTTER COOKIES

MAKES ABOUT 3½ DOZEN

½ cup ground almonds
½ cup sugar
½ cup all-purpose flour, sifted
1 teaspoon vanilla
½ teaspoon almond extract
2 egg whites
½ cup butter
sliced blanched almonds

1. Preheat oven to 350°F. Lightly grease 2 or 3 cookie sheets.

2. Combine ground almonds, sugar, flour, vanilla and almond extract in medium-size bowl, stirring with fork until well blended; set aside.

3. Beat egg whites with fork until foamy; stir into ground almond mixture until thoroughly combined.

4. Heat butter in small saucepan over low heat just until melted; do not allow the butter to foam. Remove from heat and gradually pour melted butter into almond mixture, beating constantly with wooden spoon until butter is thoroughly combined. Cover bowl and refrigerate about 15 minutes.

5. Remove from refrigerator and spoon mixture into large pastry bag fitted with No. 9 or 10 plain writing tip.

6. Pipe 2- to 3-inch fingers of dough onto prepared cookie sheets, spacing them about 2 inches apart.

7. Bake 4 to 5 minutes. Remove from oven and sprinkle sliced almonds on top of each cookie. Lightly press almonds into cookies and return to oven. Bake 5 to 6 minutes, or until edges of cookies are golden brown.

8. Remove from cookie sheets with long, thin spatula and place on wire racks to cool and crisp.

HINTS AND TIPS

To fill the pastry bag with the dough, slide the tip into the bag, making sure the tip is exposed through the opening in the bottom of the bag. Stand the bag upright in a tall glass or jar and fold down the open end of the bag to make a cuff. Spoon the dough into the bag, pushing it down with a rubber spatula. Twist the bag to close and pipe the cookies. As bag is gently squeezed, the dough will flow out of the tip.

PALMIERS

MAKES ABOUT 3 DOZEN

1 package (17¼ ounces) frozen
    puff pastry, thawed
sugar

1. Sprinkle work surface heavily with sugar. Place 1 sheet of pastry on sugared surface, unfold, and lay out flat. Brush pastry lightly with water and sprinkle with about 2 tablespoons sugar. Gently roll out pastry to 10 × 12-inch rectangle.

2. Trim pastry edges so they are straight. Sprinkle pastry with sugar. Draw a line with back of knife across center of dough crosswise. Roll edge of dough nearest you toward center line, making a sausage roll. Turn pastry all the way around and roll second edge to center line so the 2 rolls meet. Gently press rolls together and sprinkle with more sugar. Wrap with waxed paper and refrigerate about 1 hour. Repeat with second sheet of pastry.

3. Preheat oven to 400°F. Remove rolls from refrigerator, unwrap and slice crosswise into ½-inch thick slices. Dip the slices in sugar and place on ungreased cookie sheets, spacing them about 1½ inches apart. Slightly flatten each slice on both sides with back of spoon. Place cookie sheet on top oven rack and bake 5 to 7 minutes, or until bottoms are lightly browned. Turn Palmiers over with spatula and bake 5 to 7 minutes, or until sugar has caramelized and Palmiers are deep golden brown. Remove from cookie sheets immediately with spatula and cool completely on wire racks.

1. Roll up long edges of pastry toward center line to make 2 connected sausage rolls.

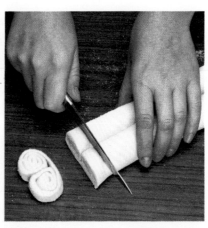

2. Cut rolls into ½-inch thick slices with sharp knife.

3. Slightly flatten Palmiers on each side, pressing down with back of spoon.

BRANDY SNAPS

MAKES ABOUT 2 DOZEN

COOKIES
½ cup all-purpose flour
1 teaspoon ground ginger
½ cup sugar
½ cup butter
¼ cup molasses
1 tablespoon brandy

FILLING
1 cup heavy cream
¼ cup confectioners sugar
1 to 2 tablespoons brandy

HINTS AND TIPS
Do not make these cookies on a hot humid day. If cookies spread and touch each other during baking, cut them apart with a small sharp knife before trying to remove them from the cookie sheet. If cookies do not hold their shapes when removed from the spoon handle, they probably were removed from the cookie sheet too soon. Open the cookie and roll it around the spoon handle again if the cookie is still warm. If necessary, return the cookies to a warm oven for 1 to 2 minutes. You can also roll the cookies around cannoli tubes if you want a wider opening in the cookie. It is also possible to make baskets to hold ice cream, fruit, cold pudding or mousse. Shape the cookies around the bottoms of greased muffin pans, custard cups or small ramekins. Freeze cookies if you do not plan to serve them immediately.

1. **Cookies:** Preheat oven to 325°F. Grease cookie sheet. Sift flour and ginger together; set aside. Place sugar, butter and molasses in heavy saucepan over low heat, stirring until butter is melted and sugar is dissolved. Remove from heat and stir in flour mixture until well blended and smooth. Stir in brandy.

2. Drop mixture by level teaspoonfuls onto prepared cookie sheet, making 4 to 5 cookies spaced 3 to 4 inches apart. Bake in upper third of oven 7 to 8 minutes, or until lightly browned, turning cookie sheet halfway through baking for even browning.

3. Place cookie sheet on wire rack about 1 minute. Remove cookies promptly from cookie sheet, 1 at a time, with wide metal spatula and roll each cookie loosely around handle of wooden spoon to make a cylinder; don't roll cookies tightly. Slide each cookie off spoon handle immediately and set aside to cool. Bake and shape remaining cookies in same manner. When all cookies are completely cooled, store in airtight container until ready to serve.

4. **Filling:** To serve, beat cream until thick. Add confectioners sugar and brandy and beat until firm. Spoon whipped cream into pastry bag fitted with ½-inch star tip. Insert tip halfway into a Brandy Snap and gently press pastry bag to fill half the cookie, forming a swirl or rosette at end of opening. Fill other end of cookie in same manner. Repeat with remaining cookies. Arrange filled cookies on serving plate and serve immediately. Brandy Snaps should be crisp, so fill them just before serving.

VARIATIONS
Lace Wafers: Prepare as directed above, but do not roll cookies. Remove from oven and let stand on cookie sheet 2 to 3 minutes. Cover wire racks with aluminum foil and place cookies on covered racks to cool.
Almond Lace Cookies: Prepare as directed above, omitting ginger. Add ¼ cup finely chopped almonds with flour. Proceed as directed for Lace Wafers or shape like Brandy Snaps.

HONEY-SPICE COOKIES

MAKES ABOUT 4 DOZEN

COOKIES

½ cup butter or margarine,
  softened
½ cup sugar
½ cup honey
1 egg
2½ cups all-purpose flour
1 teaspoon baking powder
½ teaspoon baking soda
¼ teaspoon salt
1 teaspoon cinnamon
½ teaspoon grated nutmeg
½ teaspoon ground allspice
¼ teaspoon ground cloves

FROSTING

2 cups confectioners sugar, sifted
1 to 2 tablespoons lemon juice,
  orange juice or water

1. Cookies: Cream butter, sugar and honey together until light and fluffy. Beat in egg.

2. Sift flour, baking powder, baking soda, salt, cinnamon, nutmeg, allspice and cloves together; stir into creamed mixture until well blended. Cover and refrigerate about 1 hour.

3. Preheat oven to 350°F. Remove dough from refrigerator and place on lightly floured surface. Roll dough out to about ¼-inch thickness. Cut dough with plain, floured 2- to 3-inch round cookie cutter. Place cookies on ungreased cookie sheets, spacing them about 1 inch apart. Bake 8 to 10 minutes, or until edges of cookies are lightly browned. Remove from cookie sheets with spatula and cool completely on wire racks.

4. Frosting: Blend confectioners sugar and juice together until smooth. Spoon a little frosting onto each cookie and spread with flat-bladed knife. Let frosting set before serving.

HINTS AND TIPS
Honey will slide out of the measuring cup quickly and easily if you grease the cup lightly before measuring the honey.

QUICK BREADS AND MUFFINS

Quick breads are quick and easy to prepare. They are ideal for the busy cook who has limited time to spend in the kitchen but who wants to make a home-baked product.

It is not necessary to knead the dough and wait for it to rise. As soon as you combine the liquid with the baking powder or baking soda, tiny little bubbles of carbon dioxide gas form, causing the batter to expand and make the bread light and tender.

Quick breads are suitable for almost any occasion: easy to prepare for everyday family meals, special enough to serve at simple dinner parties, and ideal for holiday gift giving. They are delicious served with sweet creamy butter, homemade jam or softened cream cheese.

Many quick breads are laden with fruit or nuts that make them sweet, moist and delicious. Their flavor improves when the bread is wrapped and stored for a day, and the bread will be easier to slice the day after it is made than it would be when fresh.

HINTS AND TIPS FOR MAKING QUICK BREADS AND MUFFINS

● Assemble all ingredients and allow them to come to room temperature before mixing batter. (Butter should be allowed to soften, but should not come to room temperature.)
● Preheat the oven for at least 10 to 15 minutes.
● Bake breads and muffins in the center of the oven.
● Stagger pans so they are not placed directly over each other. Make sure the pans don't touch each other or the oven walls.
● Thoroughly grease the pans.
● Fill the pans about half full to allow enough room for the bread or muffins to expand during baking.
● Don't overmix the batter. Mix just until all the dry ingredients are well moistened. Lumpy batter is correct.
● Test for doneness after the minimum baking time by inserting a toothpick or cake tester in the center of the bread. If it comes out clean, the bread is done.
● Cool the bread in the pan on a wire rack for 10 minutes before removing it from the pan. Remove from the pan and let cool completely on a rack before serving.
● To store, wrap cooled bread in plastic wrap or aluminum foil and store at room temperature to improve flavor.
● To freeze, wrap cooled bread in plastic wrap or aluminum foil and place in a plastic freezer bag. Tie securely, label and date. Freeze for up to three months. To serve, thaw, wrapped, at room temperature.
● Don't worry if there is a crack down the center of the bread—it belongs there.

Clockwise: Whole-Wheat Molasses Bread (page 141), Buttermilk-Blueberry Muffins (page 137), Quick Sugar and Spice Rolls (page 138)

DATE AND WALNUT BREAD

MAKES 1 LOAF

1¾ cups all-purpose flour
1 cup sugar
2 teaspoons baking powder
1 teaspoon baking soda
½ teaspoon salt
1 cup pitted dates, coarsely
chopped
1 cup coarsely chopped walnuts
1 egg
1 teaspoon vanilla
¼ cup butter or margarine, melted
and cooled
¾ cup milk

1. Preheat oven to 350°F. Grease 9 × 5-inch loaf pan.

2. Stir flour, sugar, baking powder, baking soda and salt together in large bowl. Add dates and nuts; stir until well coated.

3. Beat egg, vanilla, butter and milk together in small bowl with wire whisk or fork until well blended.

4. Make well in center of dry ingredients and stir in beaten egg mixture with wooden spoon until dry ingredients are well blended and moistened. Pour batter into prepared pan.

5. Bake in center of oven about 1 hour, or until toothpick inserted in center comes out clean.

6. Cool in pan on wire rack 10 minutes. Invert from pan and cool completely on rack.

BANANA BREAD

MAKES 1 LOAF

1¾ cups all-purpose flour
1½ teaspoons baking powder
½ teaspoon baking soda
½ teaspoon salt
½ teaspoon ground ginger
¼ teaspoon ground allspice
¼ teaspoon grated nutmeg
1 teaspoon grated lemon peel
  (optional)
¼ cup ground almonds (optional)
½ cup butter or margarine
¾ cup sugar
2 eggs
1½ cups mashed bananas (4
  medium-size bananas)

1. Preheat oven to 350°F. Grease 9 × 5-inch loaf pan.

2. Sift flour, baking powder, baking soda, salt, ginger, allspice and nutmeg together in bowl. Add lemon peel and almonds; stir until combined. Set aside.

3. Beat butter in large mixing bowl until soft and creamy. Beat in sugar until light and fluffy. Add eggs and beat until thoroughly blended. Beat in flour mixture alternately with bananas until mixture is well blended. Pour into prepared pan.

4. Bake in center of oven 1 hour to 1 hour 5 minutes, or until toothpick inserted in center comes out clean.

5. Cool in pan on wire rack 10 minutes. Invert from pan and cool completely on rack.

VARIATION
Banana-Pecan or Banana-Walnut Bread: Prepare as directed above, omitting almonds. Add ¾ cup coarsely chopped pecans or walnuts with bananas.

FRUITY TEA BREAD

MAKES 1 LOAF

1 cup golden raisins
1 cup currants or dark raisins
1 cup firmly packed light brown
   sugar
1 cup strong brewed tea or warm
   water
2½ cups all-purpose flour
3 teaspoons baking powder
1 teaspoon cinnamon
½ teaspoon salt
½ teaspoon ground allspice
¼ teaspoon grated nutmeg
2 eggs
¼ cup vegetable oil
2 tablespoons honey (optional)

1. Place raisins, currants and brown sugar in bowl. Pour tea over fruit and stir well. Let mixture stand several hours or overnight.

2. Preheat oven to 350°F. Grease 9 x 5-inch loaf pan.

3. Sift flour, baking powder, cinnamon, salt, allspice and nutmeg together in large bowl.

4. Beat eggs and oil together until well blended. Pour into fruit-tea mixture and stir until well combined. Pour fruit-tea mixture over dry ingredients and stir until well blended and moistened. Pour into prepared pan.

5. Bake in center of oven 55 to 60 minutes, or until toothpick inserted in center comes out clean.

6. Cool in pan on wire rack 10 minutes. Invert from pan and cool completely on rack.

7. Warm honey in small saucepan over low heat. Remove from heat and brush honey generously over top of bread. Let stand 10 minutes to set, then cut into thick slices and serve with sweet creamy butter.

BUTTERMILK-BLUEBERRY MUFFINS

MAKES 1 DOZEN

2 cups all-purpose flour
½ cup sugar
2½ teaspoons baking powder
½ teaspoon baking soda
½ teaspoon salt
1 teaspoon grated lemon peel
1 cup buttermilk
1 egg, beaten
⅓ cup vegetable oil
1 cup blueberries
sugar

HINTS AND TIPS

The secret to making perfect muffins is in the mixing. Once liquid ingredients have been added, stir quickly and lightly to just moisten. Batter should be somewhat lumpy. Over-beaten batter causes muffins to be tough.

1. Preheat oven to 400°F. Grease 12-cup muffin pan.

2. Stir flour, sugar, baking powder, baking soda, salt and lemon peel together in large bowl until well combined.

3. Combine buttermilk, egg and vegetable oil until well blended. Make well in center of dry ingredients and pour in buttermilk mixture. Stir with wooden spoon just until dry ingredients are moistened; batter will be lumpy. Fold in blueberries.

4. Spoon batter into prepared muffin cups, filling them about three-quarters full. Sprinkle with sugar.

5. Bake 20 to 25 minutes, or until golden.

6. Remove immediately from pan to wire rack. Serve piping hot with lots of sweet butter.

VARIATION

Blueberry-Apple Muffins: Omit baking soda and increase baking powder to 3 teaspoons. Stir ½ teaspoon cinnamon into dry ingredients. Substitute 1 cup milk for buttermilk. Use only ½ to ¾ cup blueberries and add 1 cup chopped apples.

QUICK SUGAR AND SPICE ROLLS

MAKES 12 ROLLS

ROLLS
2 cups all-purpose flour
3 tablespoons sugar
1 teaspoon baking powder
½ teaspoon salt
⅓ cup butter or margarine
½ cup milk
2 tablespoons butter, melted

FILLING
⅓ cup firmly packed light brown
  sugar
½ cup chopped walnuts or pecans
2 tablespoons golden or dark
  raisins, chopped
¾ teaspoon cinnamon
½ teaspoon ground allspice
1 egg yolk, beaten with
  1 tablespoon milk

1. **Rolls:** Preheat oven to 425°F. Lightly grease cookie sheet.

2. Stir flour, sugar, baking powder and salt together in bowl. Cut in butter until mixture is consistency of coarse crumbs. Make well in center of dry ingredients and pour in milk. Stir until mixture binds together.

3. Place dough on well-floured surface and knead about 1 minute, or until smooth. Shape dough into flattened round. Roll dough out to 10 × 12-inch rectangle and trim edges with sharp knife.

4. Brush dough generously with melted butter.

5. **Filling:** Combine brown sugar, nuts, raisins, cinnamon and allspice; sprinkle over dough to within ¼ inch of edges.

6. Starting from long end, roll up dough, jelly-roll style; pinch seam to seal.

7. Brush roll with some of the beaten egg yolk mixture and cut into 12 slices. Arrange slices on prepared cookie sheet and flatten each slice with heel of hand or rolling pin.

8. Lightly brush each slice with remaining beaten egg yolk mixture.

9. Bake 15 to 18 minutes, or until golden brown.

10. Remove rolls from cookie sheet to wire rack, and cool 10 minutes. Serve warm.

VARIATION
Coffee Ring: Arrange slices slightly overlapping each other in circle on prepared cookie sheet. Bake as directed above. Cool on cookie sheet on wire rack 10 minutes. Carefully remove from cookie sheet with wide spatula to wire rack to cool completely or serve warm.

CHEESY-NUT BREAD

MAKES 1 LOAF

1 cup all-purpose flour
1 cup whole-wheat flour
3 teaspoons baking powder
1 cup sugar
½ teaspoon salt
1 egg
¼ cup vegetable oil
1 cup milk
1 cup grated Cheddar cheese
½ cup chopped walnuts or pecans

1. Preheat oven to 350°F. Grease 9 × 5-inch loaf pan.

2. Stir flours, baking powder, sugar and salt together in bowl; set aside.

3. Beat egg, oil and milk together until well blended. Make well in center of dry ingredients and stir in beaten egg mixture just until dry ingredients are moistened. Stir in cheese and nuts. Pour into prepared pan.

4. Bake in center of oven 45 minutes, or until toothpick inserted in center comes out clean.

5. Cool in pan on wire rack 10 minutes. Invert from pan and cool slightly. Serve warm with sweet creamy butter, or cool completely.

140

WHOLE-WHEAT MOLASSES BREAD

MAKES 1 LOAF

2 cups all-purpose flour
1 cup whole-wheat flour
2 teaspoons baking powder
1 teaspoon baking soda
grated peel of 1 orange
1 teaspoon cinnamon
½ teaspoon salt
1 egg
¼ cup vegetable oil
¾ cup firmly packed dark brown
   sugar
½ cup molasses
½ cup milk
½ cup orange juice
¾ cup chopped walnuts

1. Preheat oven to 350°F. Grease 9 x 5-inch loaf pan.

2. Stir flours, baking powder, baking soda, orange peel, cinnamon and salt together in bowl; set aside.

3. Beat egg and oil together in large mixing bowl until well blended. Add brown sugar, molasses and milk; beat until well combined. Add flour mixture alternately with orange juice, beating just until dry ingredients are moistened. Stir in walnuts. Pour into prepared pan.

4. Bake in center of oven 1 hour to 1 hour 10 minutes, or until toothpick inserted in center comes out clean.

5. Cool in pan on wire rack 10 minutes. Invert from pan and cool completely on rack.

CORN BREAD

SERVES 9

1 cup all-purpose flour
1 cup cornmeal
3 to 4 tablespoons sugar
3 teaspoons baking powder
1 teaspoon salt
2 eggs
1 cup milk
¼ cup butter or margarine, melted

1. Preheat oven to 425°F. Grease 8-inch square baking pan.

2. Stir flour, cornmeal, sugar, baking powder and salt together in large mixing bowl until well blended.

3. Beat eggs, milk and melted butter together until well combined. Make well in center of dry ingredients and pour in milk mixture. Stir with wooden spoon just until dry ingredients are moistened. Pour into prepared pan. Bake 20 to 25 minutes, or until top is golden brown.

4. Serve hot, cut into squares, with lots of butter.

VARIATIONS

Corn Muffins (makes 12 muffins): Grease 12-cup muffin pan. Prepare corn bread as directed above and spoon batter into prepared muffin cups, filling them about two-thirds full. Bake 15 to 20 minutes, or until tops are golden brown. Remove from pan and serve piping hot.

Corn Sticks (makes 14 corn sticks): Thoroughly grease 2 corn stick pans and place in oven while oven is preheating. Prepare corn bread as directed above. Remove pans from oven and spoon batter into hot pans, filling each mold about three-quarters full. Bake 15 to 20 minutes, or until lightly browned. Remove from pans and serve hot.

Buttermilk Corn Bread: Stir ¾ teaspoon baking soda into dry ingredients. Substitute 1 cup buttermilk for milk.

Bacon Corn Bread: Decrease salt to ½ teaspoon. Add 6 slices cooked and crumbled bacon along with milk. (Bacon fat may be used in place of melted butter, if desired.)

Tex-Mex Corn Bread: Stir 1 teaspoon chili powder, ½ teaspoon thyme and ¼ teaspoon crushed red pepper (optional) into dry ingredients. Stir in ¼ cup finely chopped onion, 1 can (4 ounces) chopped green chilies, drained, and 1 cup shredded sharp Cheddar or monterey jack cheese along with liquid ingredients. Bake in greased 9-inch square baking pan 30 to 35 minutes. Serve hot.

Double Corn Bread: Increase baking powder to 4 teaspoons. Stir in 1 can (8 ounces) cream-style corn along with liquid ingredients. Bake in greased 9-inch square baking pan 25 to 30 minutes, or until golden brown.

BOSTON BROWN BREAD

MAKES 2 LOAVES

1 cup whole-wheat flour
1 cup rye flour
1 cup yellow or white cornmeal
2 teaspoons baking soda
1 teaspoon salt
2 cups buttermilk
¾ cup molasses
1 cup raisins (optional)

1. Thoroughly grease two 1-pound coffee cans. Cut 2 pieces of aluminum foil large enough to use as lids and grease 1 side of each piece of aluminum foil.

2. Stir flours, cornmeal, baking soda and salt together in large bowl until well combined.

3. Combine buttermilk and molasses. Make well in center of dry ingredients and pour in buttermilk mixture. Stir with wooden spoon until mixture is blended and dry ingredients are well moistened. Stir in raisins.

4. Spoon batter into prepared cans, filling each can no more than two-thirds full. Cover each can with prepared aluminum foil, greased side down. Tie aluminum foil to can with string.

5. Place filled cans on rack in large pot or Dutch oven. Pour in enough boiling water to come halfway up sides of cans. Cover pot and simmer 1½ to 2 hours, or until metal skewer inserted in center of each loaf comes out clean, adding more boiling water as necessary to maintain water level.

6. Remove cans and cool upright on wire rack 2 minutes. Remove string and aluminum foil and invert bread from cans. Cool completely on rack or serve warm. Cut into thick slices and serve with sweet creamy butter. (Delicious when served with Boston Baked Beans for a traditional New England dinner.)

145

BAKING WITH YEAST

Very few baked products provide a more tantalizing aroma than bread, rolls and cakes made with yeast. It is a fragrance that often triggers memories from childhood.

Yeast is handled in one of two ways. The conventional method is to dissolve yeast in warm water (105°F to 115°F) to which a small amount of sugar is added. This mixture is allowed to stand 5 to 10 minutes, or until foamy, and then is combined with other ingredients. The second method is the rapid mix method in which dry yeast is mixed with other dry ingredients and warmer liquid (120°F to 130°F) is added. The dough is then mixed with an electric mixer.

Baking with yeast may take a little practice, but it is less difficult than many people think. If you follow the rules for handling yeast, you will be able to bake beautiful bread and cakes in less time than you might expect.

HINTS AND TIPS FOR BAKING WITH YEAST

● Most yeast recipes call for an approximate amount of flour. This is because the amount of flour necessary to make a dough that is not sticky and is easy to handle will vary, depending on humidity and the brand of flour used. Never use more flour than necessary, or the bread will be heavy.

● Always check the expiration date on a package of yeast. Never use yeast past the expiration date.

● Measure the temperature of the liquid added to yeast with a thermometer. If the liquid is too hot, it will kill the yeast and your dough will never rise. If the liquid is too cool, the dough will rise too slowly.

● To knead dough properly, place it on a lightly floured smooth work surface (the kitchen table is an ideal height). Flour your hands lightly and push the dough down with the heels of your hands, allowing your fingers to curve over the dough. Turn dough a quarter turn, fold it over, and push down again. Repeat the pushing and folding until dough is smooth and elastic, usually about 10 minutes.

● Never place dough on a hot radiator or on top of a hot stove to rise. It won't work. There is no way you can safely reduce the time necessary for dough to rise properly. Allow the dough to rise in a warm draft-free place. The inside of a cool oven is a good choice. If the oven is very cold, preheat it to 200°F, then turn it off before placing the dough inside to rise.

● In order to find out if dough has finished rising, press it lightly with a fingertip. If the dent remains, the dough has doubled in bulk.

● If you are having trouble shaping or rolling dough, let it rest 5 or 10 minutes.

● Fill pans only two-thirds full. Allow the dough to rise only slightly above the rim of the pan in which it is to be baked.

● Preheat the oven and check with an oven thermometer to be sure you are baking at the correct temperature.

● Use the pan size called for in the recipe.

● Remove bread or cake promptly from pan and cool completely on wire rack away from drafts.

Clockwise: White Bread (page 148), Poppy Seed Roll (page 162), Potica (page 166)

WHITE BREAD

MAKES 2 LOAVES

about 5½ to 6 cups all-purpose or
 bread flour
2 tablespoons sugar
2½ teaspoons salt
1 package active dry yeast
2 cups milk
¼ cup butter or margarine

GLAZE
1 egg, beaten with 1 tablespoon
 water

RAPID-MIX METHOD

1. Combine 2 cups flour, sugar, salt and yeast in large mixing bowl. Place milk and butter in heavy saucepan and heat until warm (120°F to 130°F), stirring constantly. Gradually add warm milk mixture to flour mixture, beating at low speed. Beat 1 minute. Add ½ to ¾ cup flour or enough flour to make thick batter. Beat 3 minutes at high speed. Stir in as much remaining flour as possible with wooden spoon to make soft dough.

2. Place dough on lightly floured surface and knead in as much remaining flour as necessary to make a stiff dough. Continue kneading about 10 minutes, or until dough is smooth and elastic.

3. Place in greased bowl and turn to coat entire surface. Cover with clean towel and let rise in warm, draft-free place about 1 hour, or until doubled in bulk. Grease two 9 × 5-inch loaf pans. Punch dough down and divide in half. Shape each half into a loaf and place, seam side down, in prepared pans. Cover and let rise in warm, draft-free place about 45 minutes, or until dough is slightly above rims of pans.

4. Preheat oven to 375°F. Lightly brush tops of loaves with beaten egg glaze. Bake 35 to 40 minutes, or until loaves sound hollow when tapped on bottom. Remove from pans and cool on wire racks.

MAKES 2 LOAVES

1 package active dry yeast
2 tablespoons plus 1 teaspoon
 sugar
¼ cup warm water (110°F to
 115°F)
2 cups milk
¼ cup butter or margarine
2½ teaspoons salt
about 5½ to 6½ cups all-purpose
 or bread flour

GLAZE
1 egg, beaten with 1 tablespoon
 water

CONVENTIONAL METHOD

1. Place yeast and 1 teaspoon sugar in large mixing bowl and stir in warm water until yeast and sugar are dissolved. Let stand about 5 minutes, or until foamy.

2. Place milk, butter, remaining 2 tablespoons sugar and salt in heavy saucepan; heat until warm (115°F to 120°F), stirring constantly. Remove from heat and let cool to lukewarm (about 105°F). Add to yeast mixture and stir.

3. Add 2 cups flour and stir until smooth. Stir in as much remaining flour as possible with wooden spoon to make soft dough.

4. Proceed as directed above, starting at Step 2.

WHOLE-WHEAT BREAD

MAKES 2 LOAVES

4 cups all-purpose flour
3½ cups whole-wheat flour
¼ cup firmly packed dark brown
   sugar
1 tablespoon salt
2 packages active dry yeast
1½ cups milk
⅓ cup molasses
⅓ cup butter or margarine
3 tablespoons cracked wheat cereal
   (optional)

1. Combine flours in bowl and stir well.

2. Measure 2 cups flour mixture and place in large mixing bowl. Add brown sugar, salt and yeast; stir until well combined.

3. Place milk, 1 cup water, molasses and butter in heavy saucepan; heat until warm (120°F to 130°F), stirring constantly. Gradually add warm milk mixture to flour-yeast mixture, beating at low speed. Increase speed to medium and beat 2 minutes. Add ½ to ¾ cup flour mixture or enough flour to make thick batter. Beat at high speed 2 minutes. Stir in as much remaining flour mixture as possible with wooden spoon to make a soft dough.

4. Place dough on lightly floured surface and knead in as much remaining flour mixture as necessary to make a stiff dough. Continue kneading about 10 minutes, or until dough is smooth and elastic. Place in greased bowl and turn to coat entire surface. Cover with clean towel and let rise in warm, draft-free place about 1½ to 2 hours, or until doubled in bulk.

5. Grease two 9 × 5-inch loaf pans. Sprinkle 1 tablespoon cracked wheat cereal inside each pan, coating sides and bottoms of pans. Punch dough down and divide in half. Shape each half into a loaf and place, seam side down, in prepared pans. Cover and let rise in warm, draft-free place about 1 hour, or until dough is slightly above rims of pans.

6. Preheat oven to 375°F. Lightly brush tops of loaves with water. Sprinkle remaining cracked wheat cereal over top of each loaf. Bake 35 to 40 minutes, or until loaves sound hollow when tapped on bottom. Remove from pans and cool on wire racks.

VARIATION

To make a loaf of bread entirely with whole-wheat flour, use 7½ cups whole-wheat flour and omit all-purpose flour. Use 2½ cups milk and omit the water. However, bread made with dark flour only tends to be dry, rises less, and takes a longer time to rise than bread that contains some white flour.

SWEDISH RYE BREAD

MAKES 2 LOAVES

about 3½ to 4 cups all-purpose
 flour
¼ cup firmly packed dark brown
 sugar
2 teaspoons salt
1 package active dry yeast
¼ cup butter or margarine
¼ cup molasses
2½ cups medium rye flour

GLAZE
1 egg white, beaten with
 1 tablespoon water

1. Stir 2 cups all-purpose flour, brown sugar, salt and yeast together in large mixing bowl until well combined.

2. Place 1¾ cups water, butter and molasses in heavy saucepan and heat until warm (120°F to 130°F), stirring constantly. Remove from heat and gradually add warm liquid to flour mixture, beating at low speed until well blended and smooth. Increase speed to medium and beat 2 minutes. Add ½ to ¾ cup all-purpose flour or enough flour to make thick batter. Beat at high speed 3 minutes. Stir in all of the rye flour and as much all-purpose flour as possible with wooden spoon to make soft dough.

3. Place dough on lightly floured surface and knead in as much remaining all-purpose flour as necessary to make stiff dough. Continue kneading about 10 minutes, or until dough is smooth and elastic. Place in greased bowl and turn to coat entire surface. Cover with clean towel and let rise in warm, draft-free place about 1½ to 2 hours, or until doubled in bulk.

4. Grease large cookie sheet. Punch dough down and divide in half. Cover and let rest 10 to 15 minutes. Shape each half into a smooth round ball, pinching and tucking ends under. Place balls at opposite ends of prepared cookie sheet. Flatten each ball slightly with palm of hand or lightly pat balls with fingertips to flatten. Cover and let rise in a warm, draft-free place about 1 hour, or until doubled in bulk.

5. Preheat oven to 375°F. Bake loaves 20 minutes. Remove loaves from oven and brush tops with egg white glaze. Return loaves to oven and bake 15 to 20 minutes, or until bottoms of loaves sound hollow when lightly tapped. Remove from cookie sheet immediately and cool on wire racks.

VARIATION
Caraway Rye Bread: Stir 2 tablespoons caraway seed into flour-yeast mixture and proceed as directed above. Brush loaves with egg glaze and sprinkle top of each loaf with additional caraway seed, if desired.

FRENCH BREAD

MAKES 3 LOAVES

2 packages active dry yeast
2 teaspoons sugar
2¼ cups warm water (105°F to 115°F)
about 6½ to 7 cups all-purpose flour
1 tablespoon salt
cornmeal

1. Place yeast and sugar in large mixing bowl. Add warm water and stir until yeast and sugar are dissolved. Let stand 5 to 10 minutes, or until foamy.

2. Add 2 cups flour and salt to bowl; stir with wooden spoon until smooth. Stir in as much remaining flour as possible, 1 cup at a time, to make stiff dough.

3. Place dough on lightly floured surface and knead in as much flour as necessary to make fairly stiff dough. Continue kneading about 8 to 10 minutes, or until dough is smooth and elastic. Place dough in greased bowl and turn to coat entire surface. Cover with clean towel and let rise in warm, draft-free place about 1 to 1½ hours, or until doubled in bulk.

4. Grease a large cookie sheet and lightly sprinkle cookie sheet with cornmeal. Punch dough down and place on lightly floured surface. Knead dough 2 minutes. Cut dough into three equal-size pieces. Shape each piece into a roll, about 10 inches long, tapering ends of each roll. Pinch ends to seal. Place on prepared cookie sheet, spacing them about 3 inches apart. Lightly brush each loaf with cold water. Cover and let rise in warm, draft-free place about 1 hour, or until loaves are doubled in bulk.

5. Preheat oven to 425°F. Uncover loaves and cut 3 or 4 diagonal slashes across top of each loaf with very sharp knife. Place large, shallow baking pan, half filled with hot water, on bottom rack of oven. Bake loaves 35 to 40 minutes, or until loaves are lightly browned and sound hollow when tapped on bottom. Brush or spray loaves with water every 10 minutes to give bread a nice hard crust.

VARIATION
Hard Rolls: Prepare dough and let rise until doubled, as directed above. Punch dough down and divide in half. Cut each half into 12 equal-size pieces. Shape each piece into a slightly flattened ball, pinching and tucking ends under. Grease 2 cookie sheets and sprinkle cookie sheets with cornmeal. Place rolls on cookie sheets, spacing them about 2 inches apart. Brush top of each roll with cold water. Cover and let rise in warm, draft-free place about 50 to 60 minutes, or until doubled in bulk. Uncover rolls and cut an "X" in top of each roll with very sharp knife or pair of scissors. Brush with water. Bake 20 to 25 minutes, or until rolls sound hollow when tapped on bottom. Remove from cookie sheets and cool on wire rack. Makes 2 dozen rolls.

1. Knead dough on a lightly floured surface about 8 to 10 minutes, or until smooth and elastic.

2. Place dough in greased bowl and turn to coat entire surface. Cover with clean towel and let rise in warm, draft-free place 1 to 1½ hours, or until doubled.

3. Punch dough down and knead lightly about 2 minutes, or until dough is smooth and free of air bubbles.

4. Cut dough crosswise with very sharp knife into 3 equal pieces.

5. Shape each piece of dough into a roll, about 10 inches long, tapering the ends of each roll. Place on prepared cookie sheet and let rise in warm, draft-free place about 1 hour, or until doubled.

6. Preheat oven to 425°F. Cut 3 or 4 diagonal slashes across top of each loaf with very sharp knife. Place large, shallow baking pan, half filled with hot water, on bottom rack of oven.

7. Bake 35 to 40 minutes, or until loaves are lightly browned and sound hollow when tapped on bottom. Brush or spray with water every 10 minutes to give bread a nice hard crust.

STRIZEL BRAIDED LOAF

MAKES 1 LARGE LOAF

about 3½ cups all-purpose flour
1 package active dry yeast
½ cup milk
2 tablespoons butter or margarine
¼ cup sugar
1 teaspoon salt
2 eggs
2 teaspooons grated lemon peel
½ teaspoon cinnamon
½ teaspoon ground coriander
1 cup raisins
¼ cup chopped mixed candied fruit

GLAZE
1 egg, beaten with 1 tablespoon
   milk

1. Combine 1½ cups flour and yeast in large mixing bowl.

2. Place milk, ¼ cup water, butter, sugar and salt in heavy saucepan over low heat and heat until warm (120°F to 130°F), stirring constantly. Gradually add to flour mixture, beating at low speed until well blended. Beat in eggs. Add ½ cup flour, lemon peel, cinnamon and coriander; beat at high speed 2 minutes. Stir in raisins and candied fruit. Stir in as much remaining flour as possible with wooden spoon to make soft dough.

3. Place dough on lightly floured surface and knead in as much remaining flour as necessary to make moderately stiff dough. Continue kneading about 8 to 10 minutes, or until dough is smooth and elastic. Place dough in greased bowl and turn to coat entire surface. Cover with clean towel and let rise in warm, draft-free place about 1 hour, or until doubled in bulk.

4. Grease large cookie sheet. Punch dough down and divide into 9 equal-size pieces. Shape each piece into a rope about 14 inches long. Place 4 ropes on prepared cookie sheet and braid, treating 2 ropes as one, and pinching and tucking ends under. Braid 3 more ropes together and place on top of first braid, pinching and tucking ends under. Twist remaining 2 ropes together and place on top of loaf. Cover with clean towel and let rise in warm, draft-free place about 1 hour, or until almost doubled in bulk.

5. Preheat oven to 375°F. Brush egg glaze over braided loaf. Bake 30 to 35 minutes, or until nicely browned. Remove from cookie sheet to cool on wire rack.

RUM SAVARIN

CAKE
1 package active dry yeast
2 tablespoons sugar
¼ cup warm water (105°F to
  115°F)
2 cups all-purpose flour
½ teaspoon salt
2 eggs, beaten
¼ cup milk
⅓ cup butter or margarine, melted
  and cooled

RUM SYRUP
1 cup sugar
½ to ⅓ cup dark rum

GLAZE AND FILLING
½ cup apricot jam
2 tablespoons dark rum
1 cup heavy cream
2 tablespoons confectioners sugar
1 teaspoon vanilla
sliced strawberries, bananas,
  peaches or other fresh fruit in
  season

1. Cake: Lightly grease 9-inch (6½ cup) ring mold or savarin mold. Sprinkle yeast and 1 teaspooon sugar over warm water in bowl; stir to dissolve. Let stand 5 to 10 minutes, or until foamy.

2. Stir in 1 cup flour, salt and remaining sugar with wooden spoon until well blended. Add beaten eggs, remaining 1 cup flour and milk; beat vigorously until very smooth. Stir in melted butter until well blended.

3. Spoon batter into prepared mold. Cover with clean towel and let rise in warm, draft-free place about 1 to 1½ hours, or until dough almost reaches rim of mold.

4. Preheat oven to 375°F. Bake 30 to 35 minutes, or until top is browned. Invert from mold onto wire rack.

5. Rum Syrup: Place sugar and 1½ cups water in saucepan and bring to a boil, stirring until sugar is dissolved. Boil gently 5 minutes without stirring. Remove from heat and cool slightly. Stir in rum.

6. While savarin is still warm, place, rounded side up, in large, deep serving plate. Prick all over with metal skewer or fork. Spoon warm rum syrup over top and let stand about 1 hour, basting frequently, until all syrup has been absorbed.

7. Glaze and Filling: Press jam through strainer into small saucepan and stir in 1 tablespoon water. Heat until jam is melted. Remove from heat and cool slightly. Stir in rum. Brush apricot glaze over savarin, covering it completely. Refrigerate until ready to serve.

8. To serve, beat cream until thick. Add confectioners sugar and vanilla; beat until firm. Spoon whipped cream into pastry bag fitted with medium-size star tip. Pipe some whipped cream in center of savarin and arrange sliced fruit on top of whipped cream. Pipe a border of whipped cream around bottom edge of savarin and around fruit.

BRIOCHE

MAKES 1 LARGE OR 24 SMALL BRIOCHES

½ cup milk
2 packages active dry yeast
¼ cup sugar
¼ cup warm water (105°F to 115°F)
4½ cups all-purpose flour
1 teaspoon salt
1 cup butter or margarine, softened
5 eggs
melted butter

GLAZE
1 egg, beaten with 1 tablespoon milk

HINTS AND TIPS
When brushing the brioche with the egg glaze, be careful not to let the glaze run into the hole where the two balls are connected. It will prevent the smaller ball from rising during baking. When making individual brioches, shape 4 or 5 pieces of dough at a time. Cover and refrigerate the remaining dough until you are ready to shape it. Don't try to beat the dough with a hand-held electric mixer—it doesn't have enough power. (If you use an electric mixer, you must use a heavy-duty model.) The dough can be beaten with a wooden spoon, a strong arm and a lot of energy. If you don't have 24 individual brioche pans, use 2 greased 12-cup muffin pans.

1. Scald ½ cup milk and set aside to cool.

2. Dissolve yeast and 1 teaspoon sugar in warm water. Let stand 5 to 10 minutes, or until foamy.

3. Place 2 cups flour, remaining sugar and salt in large mixing bowl. Pour in yeast mixture and cooled milk; beat at low speed until well blended. Beat in butter until well blended. Beat in 1½ cups flour and eggs, 1 at a time, beating well after each addition. Beat 2 minutes. Beat in remaining 1 cup flour and continue beating at medium speed about 8 to 10 minutes, or until dough is shiny. Cover and let rise in warm, draft-free place about 2 hours, or until doubled in bulk.

4. Stir dough down with wooden spoon. Cover tightly with aluminum foil or plastic wrap and refrigerate overnight.

5. To shape dough, remove from refrigerator and punch dough down. Place on lightly floured surface and knead 2 minutes.

6. Grease 9-inch wide brioche mold. Pinch off one-fifth of dough (about the size of a small apple) and set aside. Shape large piece of dough into a smooth ball and place in prepared mold. Shape smaller piece of dough into a ball with a point at 1 end. Press index finger into center of larger ball to make a hole about two-thirds of the way through dough. Place smaller ball, pointed end down, into hole of larger ball and press down lightly. Brush top of brioche with melted butter, cover with large piece of waxed paper and let rise in a warm, draft-free place about 40 to 50 minutes, or until almost doubled in bulk.

7. Preheat oven to 350°F. Brush brioche with egg glaze and bake in center of oven 45 to 50 minutes, or until golden brown. Remove from pan immediately and cool on wire rack. Serve warm or cool.

VARIATION
Individual Brioches: Prepare brioche dough as directed above and let rise overnight in refrigerator. Grease 24 small brioche molds. Cut off one-quarter of dough; set aside. Cut remaining piece of dough into 24 equal-size pieces. Shape each piece in a smooth ball and place in prepared molds. Cut smaller piece of dough into 24 pieces and shape each piece into a small ball with a pointed end. Make a hole in larger balls and attach small balls as above. Cover and let rise in warm, draft-free place about 50 minutes, or until doubled in bulk. Brush with egg glaze. Bake in 425°F oven 10 to 15 minutes, or until nicely browned. Remove from pans immediately and cool on wire racks.

POPPY SEED ROLL

MAKES 1 COFFEE CAKE

COFFEE CAKE
about 4 cups all-purpose flour
1 package active dry yeast
¾ cup milk
½ cup butter or margarine
½ cup sugar
1 teaspoon salt
3 eggs, beaten
2 teaspoons grated lemon peel

FILLING
1 cup poppy seed, ground
1 cup chopped pitted dates
½ cup finely chopped almonds
½ cup currants
2 teaspoons grated orange peel
1 cup sugar
1 tablespoon all-purpose flour
¼ cup butter or margarine
⅓ cup heavy cream
1 egg

GLAZE
1 egg, beaten with 1 tablespoon
  milk

1. Coffee cake: Combine 1½ cups flour and yeast in large mixing bowl.

2. Place milk, butter, sugar and salt in heavy saucepan over low heat and heat until warm (120°F to 130°F). Gradually add to flour mixture, beating at low speed until well blended. Beat in eggs. Add ½ cup flour and lemon peel; beat at high speed 2 minutes. Stir in as much remaining flour as possible with wooden spoon to make soft dough.

3. Place dough on lightly floured surface and knead in as much remaining flour as necessary to make a moderately stiff dough. Continue kneading about 10 minutes, or until dough is smooth and elastic. Place dough in greased bowl and turn to coat entire surface. Cover with clean towel and let rise in warm, draft-free place about 1 to 1½ hours, or until doubled in bulk.

4. Filling: Place poppy seed, dates, almonds, currants, orange peel, sugar and flour in bowl; toss until well coated. Melt butter in medium-size saucepan over low heat. Beat cream and egg together with fork until blended. Stir into saucepan with wire whisk until blended. Add poppy seed mixture and stir until well combined. Cook over low heat 3 minutes, stirring constantly. Remove from heat and set aside to cool.

5. Grease large cookie sheet. Punch dough down. Roll out dough on lightly floured surface to 14 × 16-inch rectangle. Spread poppy seed mixture evenly over dough to within ½ inch of edges. Starting at short end, roll up dough, jelly-roll style, to center of rectangle. Turn dough around and roll up other short side so rolls meet in middle. Lightly pinch rolls together to seal. Carefully lift roll and place, seam side down, on prepared cookie sheet. Cover and let rise in warm, draft-free place about 40 to 50 minutes, or until almost doubled in bulk.

6. Glaze: Preheat oven to 375°F. Brush glaze over roll. Bake 35 to 40 minutes, or until golden brown. Cool completely on wire rack.

SWEDISH NUT TEA RING

MAKES 2 COFFEE CAKES

COFFEE CAKE
about 4½ cups all-purpose flour
1 package active dry yeast
1¼ cups milk
¼ cup butter or margarine
½ cup sugar
1 teaspoon salt
2 eggs, beaten

FILLING
3 tablespoons butter or margarine, melted
¾ cup chopped walnuts
½ cup chopped hazelnuts or almonds
¼ cup chopped Brazil nuts
¾ cup granulated sugar
2 teaspoons cinnamon

GLAZE AND DECORATION
2 cups sifted confectioners sugar
½ teaspoon vanilla
2 to 3 tablespoons milk or light cream
red candied cherries
walnut halves

1. Coffee cake: Combine 2 cups flour and yeast in large mixing bowl.

2. Place milk, butter, sugar and salt in heavy saucepan over low heat and heat until warm (120°F to 130°F), stirring constantly. Gradually add to flour mixture, beating at low speed until blended. Add eggs and beat at high speed 2 minutes. Stir in as much remaining flour as possible, 1 cup at a time, with wooden spoon to make soft dough.

3. Place dough on lightly floured surface and knead in as much remaining flour as necessary until dough is no longer sticky. Continue kneading about 10 minutes, or until dough is smooth and elastic. Place in greased bowl and turn to coat entire surface. Cover with clean towel and let rise in warm, draft-free place about 1 hour, or until doubled in bulk. Grease 2 cookie sheets.

4. Filling: Punch dough down and divide in half. Roll out each half to 12 × 18-inch rectangle. Brush with melted butter. Combine walnuts, hazelnuts, Brazil nuts, sugar and cinnamon. Sprinkle half of nut mixture evenly over each piece to within ½ inch of edges. Starting at long end, roll up each half, jelly-roll style, pinching seams to seal.

5. Place rolls on prepared cookie sheets, seam side down. Bring 2 ends together to form rings, pinching ends to seal. Snip each ring at 1-inch intervals with scissors, cutting almost to center of ring. Turn each slice on its side. Cover and let rise in warm, draft-free place about 40 to 50 minutes, or until doubled in bulk.

6. Preheat oven to 350°F. Bake 30 to 35 minutes, or until golden brown. Remove from cookie sheets and cool on wire racks.

7. Glaze and Decoration: Combine confectioners sugar, vanilla and milk and stir until glaze is smooth and good pouring consistency. Spoon glaze over rings while they are still warm. Decorate with candied cherries and walnut halves. Let stand until glaze is set.

VARIATIONS
Currant or Raisin Tea Ring: Prepare and roll out dough as directed above. Brush with melted butter. Combine 2 cups currants or raisins, ¾ cup firmly packed brown sugar, 1 tablespoon grated orange peel and 2 teaspoons cinnamon. Sprinkle evenly over each half of dough. Roll up, bake and glaze as directed above.
Pecan Tea Ring: Prepare and roll out dough as directed above. Brush with melted butter. Combine 1½ cups chopped pecans, ¾ cup firmly packed brown sugar, 1 teaspoon cinnamon and grated peel of 1 lemon. Sprinkle evenly over each half of dough. Roll up, bake and glaze as directed above.

Sugar and Spice Tea Ring: Prepare and roll out dough as directed above. Brush with melted butter. Combine 1½ cups firmly packed brown sugar, grated peel of 2 lemons, 1 tablespoon cinnamon, 1 teaspoon grated nutmeg and ½ teaspoon ground cloves. Sprinkle evenly over each half of dough. Roll up, bake and glaze as directed above.

Almond-Fruit Ring: Prepare and roll out dough as directed above. Brush with melted butter. Combine ½ cup slivered almonds, 1 cup golden raisins, ½ cup chopped mixed candied fruit, ¼ cup sugar, 1 teaspoon cinnamon and ½ teaspoon grated nutmeg. Sprinkle evenly over each half of dough. Roll up, bake and glaze as directed above. Dough can also be filled with your favorite canned filling.

POTICA

MAKES 2 COFFEE CAKES

COFFEE CAKE
about 4 cups all-purpose flour
⅓ cup sugar
1 package active dry yeast
1 teaspoon salt
1 cup milk
½ cup butter or margarine
2 egg yolks

FILLING
2 cups very finely chopped walnuts
⅓ cup firmly packed light brown
   sugar
1 teaspoon cinnamon
grated peel of 1 lemon
grated peel of 1 orange
2 egg whites

GLAZE
milk
¼ cup honey, warmed
walnut halves (optional)
candied cherries (optional)

1. **Coffee cake:** Combine 1½ cups flour, sugar, yeast and salt in large mixing bowl.

2. Place milk and butter in heavy saucepan over low heat and heat until warm (120°F to 130°F), stirring constantly. Gradually add warm milk mixture to flour mixture. Beat at low speed about 2 minutes, or until smooth. Add egg yolks and ½ cup flour, or enough flour to make thick batter. Beat at high speed 3 minutes, scraping sides of bowl occasionally. Stir in as much remaining flour as possible with wooden spoon to make soft dough.

3. Place dough on lightly floured surface and knead in any remaining flour as necessary until dough is no longer sticky. Continue kneading about 10 minutes, or until dough is smooth and elastic. Place dough in greased bowl and turn to coat entire surface. Cover with clean towel and let rise in warm, draft-free place about 1¼ hours, or until doubled in bulk.

4. Grease 2 cookie sheets. Punch dough down and divide in half. Cover and let rest 15 minutes.

5. **Filling:** Combine walnuts, brown sugar, cinnamon and lemon and orange peels. Beat egg whites until stiff peaks form. Fold beaten whites into nut mixture.

6. Roll out each half of dough to 12 x 18-inch rectangle. Spread half of filling over each half of dough to within ½ inch of edges. Starting at short end, tightly roll up each half, jelly-roll style, pinching seams to seal. Place rolls, seam side down, on prepared cookie sheets. Shape each roll into circle or spiral. Cover and let rise in warm, draft-free place about 1 hour, or until doubled in bulk.

7. **Glaze:** Preheat oven to 350°F. Brush each roll with milk. Bake 25 to 30 minutes, or until golden brown. Remove from cookie sheet and cool on wire racks. Brush with honey and decorate with walnut halves and candied cherries.

ALMOND-RAISIN COFFEE CAKE

MAKES 1

COFFEE CAKE
about 3½ cups all-purpose flour
1 package active dry yeast
1 cup milk
½ cup butter or margarine
⅓ cup sugar
1 teaspoon salt
2 egg yolks
1 egg white, beaten with
　1 tablespoon water
vegetable oil

FILLING
½ cup sugar
1 cup raisins

DECORATION AND GLAZE
½ cup almonds, split in half
　lengthwise
1 cup confectioners sugar
1 to 2 tablespoons milk

HINTS AND TIPS

Allowing dough to rise in the refrigerator is a great time-saver. It is not necessary to wait for a first rise, shape the dough and then wait for a second rise. Simply mix the dough, shape it and refrigerate several hours or overnight. This way it is easy to make hot fresh baked coffeecake in the morning. Prepare the cake at night, refrigerate, allow to rise while you sleep, and it's ready to bake in the morning. Letting dough rest before shaping is important—it gives the yeast a chance to start working.

---

1. **Coffee cake:** Combine 1½ cups flour and yeast in large mixing bowl.

2. Place milk, butter, sugar and salt in heavy saucepan over low heat and heat until warm (120°F to 130°F). Gradually add to flour mixture, beating at low speed until well blended. Add ½ cup flour and beat at high speed 2 minutes. Beat in egg yolks. Stir in as much remaining flour as possible with wooden spoon to make a soft dough.

3. Place dough on lightly floured surface and knead in as much remaining flour as necessary to make a stiff dough. Continue kneading about 10 minutes, or until dough is smooth and elastic.

4. Cover dough with plastic wrap and then a clean towel. Let rest about 20 minutes.

5. **Filling:** Combine sugar and raisins in small bowl.

6. Roll out dough on lightly floured surface to 12 × 20-inch rectangle. Brush dough with some of the beaten egg white mixture. Reserve remaining egg white mixture. Sprinkle sugar-raisin mixture evenly over dough. Starting at long end, roll up dough, jelly-roll style, and pinch to seal.

7. Place roll, seam side down, on prepared cookie sheet. Brush lightly with oil. Cover roll loosely with plastic wrap and refrigerate 4 hours or overnight.

8. When ready to bake, remove from refrigerator and carefully uncover roll. Let stand at room temperature about 10 minutes. Lightly grease a cookie sheet.

9. Preheat oven to 375°F. Brush roll with reserved egg white mixture. Lightly press almonds, cut side down, on roll. Bake 25 to 30 minutes, or until lightly browned. Remove from cookie sheet and cool on wire rack.

10. **Glaze:** Combine confectioners sugar and milk until smooth. Spoon over cake while it is still warm. Let glaze set before serving.

CROISSANTS

MAKES ABOUT 4 DOZEN

about 3½ to 4 cups all-purpose
  flour
2 packages active dry yeast
1¼ cups milk
2 tablespoons sugar
1 teaspoon salt
1½ cups sweet butter, chilled

GLAZE
1 egg, beaten with 1 tablespoon
  water

1. Combine 2 cups flour and yeast in large mixing bowl.

2. Heat milk, sugar and salt in saucepan over low heat until warm (120°F to 130°F). Gradually add to flour mixture, beating at low speed until well blended. Increase speed to medium and beat 2 minutes. Stir in as much remaining flour as possible with a wooden spoon to make a soft dough.

3. Place dough on lightly floured surface and knead in as much remaining flour as necessary to make a moderately stiff dough. Continue kneading about 5 to 8 minutes, or until dough is smooth and elastic.

4. Roll out dough on lightly floured surface to 8 × 20-inch rectangle, keeping edges of dough straight. Dot one-third of chilled butter over two-thirds of dough. Fold dough into thirds by folding unbuttered section of dough over buttered section and remaining buttered section over top. Press edges down lightly with rolling pin to seal. Roll dough out to an 8 × 20-inch rectangle, dot one-third of butter over two-thirds of dough, and fold dough into thirds. Press seams to seal. Repeat rolling, buttering and folding steps, using remaining one-third butter. Sprinkle lightly with flour, wrap with plastic wrap and refrigerate about 1 hour.

5. Remove dough from refrigerator, roll out to an 8 × 20-inch rectangle, fold dough in thirds, wrap and refrigerate 1 hour. Repeat rolling and folding process twice, refrigerating dough after each rolling and folding. After last rolling, refrigerate dough at least 3 or up to 12 hours.

6. To shape and bake croissants, cut dough in half. Return 1 half to refrigerator. Roll out remaining half on lightly floured surface to a 6 × 21-inch rectangle. Cut in half lengthwise. Cut each strip of dough into triangles, making each triangle 3 inches wide across the base. Brush some egg glaze over triangles. (Reserve remaining egg glaze.) Roll up each triangle from 3-inch wide base and place, pointed tip down, on ungreased cookie sheets, spacing them about 1 inch apart. Curve ends to make crescent shapes. Repeat with remaining half of dough. Cover loosely with plastic wrap and let rise in warm, draft-free place about 30 to 40 minutes, or until doubled in bulk.

7. Preheat oven to 425°F. Lightly brush tops of croissants with reserved egg glaze. Bake 10 to 12 minutes, or until lightly browned. Remove immediately from cookie sheets to cool on wire racks. Serve warm or cool completely.

1. Fold the dough into thirds by folding unbuttered section of dough over buttered section. Fold the remaining buttered dough over center.

2. Roll out 1 piece of the dough to a 6 × 21-inch rectangle. Cut in half lengthwise. Cut each strip into triangles, making each triangle 3 inches across.

3. Brush each triangle with beaten egg glaze. Roll up triangles from the base to the tip, and place, pointed tip down, on ungreased cookie sheets.

DANISH PASTRIES

MAKES 4 DOZEN SMALL PASTRIES OR 3 FILLED PASTRY RINGS

PASTRY DOUGH
about 4 to 4½ cups all-purpose
    flour
⅓ cup sugar
½ teaspoon salt
2 packages active dry yeast
1 cup milk
1½ cups sweet butter
2 eggs, room temperature

EGG GLAZE
1 egg
2 teaspoons sugar

DECORATIVE TOPPING
chopped nuts
candied or maraschino cherries,
    quartered

SUGAR GLAZE
½ cup confectioners sugar
½ teaspoon vanilla

1. **Pastry Dough:** Stir 2 cups flour, sugar, salt and yeast together in large mixing bowl.

2. Place milk and ½ cup butter in heavy saucepan and heat until warm (120°F to 130°F). Gradually add warm milk mixture to flour mixture, beating at low speed until blended. Add eggs and beat at medium speed 2 minutes. Add ½ to ¾ cup flour, or enough flour to make a thick batter. Beat at high speed 3 minutes. Stir in as much remaining flour as possible with wooden spoon to make soft dough.

3. Place dough on lightly floured surface and knead in as much remaining flour as necessary to make a stiff dough. Continue kneading about 10 minutes, or until dough is smooth and elastic. Shape dough into ball, cover with clean towel, and let rest on floured surface about 15 minutes.

4. Place remaining 1 cup butter between 2 large sheets of waxed paper and roll out to a 9×14-inch rectangle. Remove top sheet of waxed paper and refrigerate butter until firm.

5. Roll out dough on lightly floured surface to a 15-inch square. Remove butter from refrigerator and invert over two-thirds of dough. Peel off waxed paper.

6. Fold dough into thirds by folding unbuttered section of dough over buttered section and remaining buttered section over top. Press edges down lightly with rolling pin to seal.

7. Roll out dough to a 10×15-inch rectangle. Fold dough into thirds to make a 5×10-inch rectangle. Wrap dough lightly with plastic wrap and refrigerate 30 minutes.

8. Remove dough from refrigerator and roll out to a 10×15-inch rectangle. Fold dough into thirds to make a 5×10-inch rectangle. Wrap and refrigerate 30 minutes. Repeat rolling and folding process twice, refrigerating dough after each rolling and folding. Refrigerate dough 30 minutes after last rolling. (Keep edges of dough straight and even when rolling, and keep dough well chilled at all times.) To make small pastries, cut dough into thirds before last refrigeration.

9. **Egg Glaze:** Beat egg, sugar and 1 tablespoon water together in small bowl with fork until blended; set aside.

10. Shape pastries and fill as desired. Lightly grease 2 cookie sheets.

11. Place Danish Pastries on prepared cookie sheets, spacing them

about 1½ to 2 inches apart. Cover and let rise in warm, draft-free place about 30 minutes.

12. Decorative Topping: Preheat oven to 425°F. Brush pastries with egg glaze. Sprinkle with chopped nuts or candied cherries. Bake 10 to 12 minutes, or until golden brown. Remove from cookie sheets and cool on wire racks.

13. Sugar Glaze: Combine confectioners sugar with 1 to 2 teaspoons water and vanilla until smooth. Drizzle glaze over pastries while they are still warm.

TO MAKE SMALL PASTRIES

1. Envelopes and pinwheels: Roll out ⅓ of dough to 6 × 24-inch rectangle and brush with egg glaze. Cut dough into sixteen 3-inch squares. Spoon about 2 teaspoons desired filling (see below) into center of each square. To make envelopes, bring 4 corners to center to enclose filling and press lightly to seal. To make pinwheels, make 4 cuts in each square diagonally from each corner toward center. Fold alternate points in toward center to enclose filling. Press lightly to seal.

2. Crescents: Roll out ⅓ of dough to 8 × 24-inch rectangle and cut into twelve 4-inch squares. Cut squares in half diagonally to make triangles. Spoon filling into center of each triangle and roll up from long side.

3. Cockscombs: Cut twelve 4-inch squares as directed for crescents and spoon filling onto half of each square. Fold each square over in half and press edges together to seal. Starting at folded edge, cut 6 to 8 slashes three-fourths of the way through; do not cut all the way through to sealed edge.

4. Spirals: Roll out ⅓ of dough to 8 × 16-inch rectangle. Spread desired filling over rectangle to within ½ inch of edges. Roll up, jelly-roll style, pinching seam to seal. Cut roll into sixteen 1-inch slices.

FILLINGS FOR SMALL PASTRIES

ENOUGH TO FILL 16 PASTRIES
½ cup crushed pineapple, well drained
½ cup ricotta or cottage cheese

Pineapple – Cheese Filling
Place pineapple and cheese in container of blender or food processor and process until almost smooth.

ENOUGH TO FILL 16 PASTRIES
⅔ cup almond paste
1 tablespoon egg yolk

Almond Filling
Combine almond paste and egg yolk, stirring with fork until well blended.

174

ENOUGH TO FILL 16 PASTRIES

¼ cup butter or margarine,
  softened
2 tablespoons sugar
½ teaspoon cinnamon
½ teaspoon grated nutmeg
¼ teaspoon ground cloves
¼ cup currants

Currant-Spice Filling

Combine butter, sugar, cinnamon, nutmeg and cloves until well blended. Stir in currants.

MAKES 3 RINGS

1 recipe Danish Pastry Dough
Egg Glaze
Filling (see below)

TO MAKE FILLED DANISH RINGS

1. Divide dough into thirds and roll out one-third to 8 × 16-inch rectangle. Spread desired filling over dough to within ½ inch of edges. Starting at long end, tightly roll up dough, jelly-roll style, pinching seam to seal.

2. Place filled roll, seam side down, on greased cookie sheet. Bring ends of roll together to form a ring and press ends together to seal. Repeat with remaining two pieces of dough and remaining filling. Cover rings and let rise in warm, draft-free place about 30 minutes, or until puffy.

3. Preheat oven to 400°F. Brush filled rings with egg glaze (above). Bake 20 to 25 minutes, or until golden brown. Remove from cookie sheets and cool on wire racks.

FILLINGS FOR DANISH RINGS

ENOUGH TO FILL 3 RINGS

¾ cup apricot jam or preserves
⅓ cup finely chopped almonds

Apricot-Almond Filling

Press apricot jam through strainer into small saucepan. Place saucepan over low heat and cook, stirring until melted. Remove from heat and let cool. Stir in almonds until well blended.

ENOUGH TO FILL 3 RINGS

1 cup raisins
¼ cup sugar
2 tablespoons butter or margarine
1 teaspoon cinnamon
1 teaspoon cornstarch
½ cup finely chopped walnuts

Raisin-Walnut Filling

Place raisins, sugar, ¼ cup water and butter in heavy saucepan and bring to a boil, stirring. Lower heat and simmer 5 minutes. Add cinnamon and cornstarch; stir well. Simmer 1 minute. Spoon raisin mixture into container of blender or food processor and process until smooth. Pour mixture into bowl and stir in walnuts. Let cool.

ENOUGH TO FILL 3 RINGS

¾ cup ricotta cheese
1 egg, beaten
2 teaspoons sugar
1 teaspoon grated lemon peel
½ teaspoon vanilla

Cheese Filling

Combine cheese, egg, sugar, lemon peel and vanilla, stirring until well blended.

BAKING SHORT CUTS

MIXES, FROZEN DOUGH AND OTHER TIME SAVERS

Cake mixes, hot roll mixes, frozen bread dough, biscuit mix and even frosting mix can all be used to good advantage with just a bit of imagination. Add a pinch of this and a dash of that, and in less time than you'd believe, you will have made a treat that everyone will think kept you busy in the kitchen for hours.

HINTS AND TIPS FOR USING MIXES
● Read the instructions on the box or package carefully. Use the pan size, oven temperature and timing recommended unless recipes provide alternate instructions.
● If you live 3,500 feet or more above sea level, check package carefully for special instructions for high altitude baking.
● Preheat oven and check with oven thermometer to be sure the temperature is correct before you start baking.
● Some cake mixes have pudding added and some do not. Don't use a cake mix with pudding added unless recipe calls for it.
● There is no reason why you can't fill and frost a cake made with a cake mix in exactly the same way you would fill and frost a cake made from scratch. Keep a card file of ideas handy and keep a selection of mixes in the pantry, ready to use at a moment's notice.
● Check expiration dates on all packages. Don't buy anything past the expiration date and don't buy anything you do not expect to use before the expiration date, or you will not get satisfactory results.
● Frozen bread dough can be defrosted in a microwave oven. Loosely wrap in plastic wrap, leaving vent at one end. Microwave at 50% power 3 minutes, make ¼ turn and microwave 3 to 4 minutes, or until dough is soft. Let stand on heatproof surface 10 to 15 minutes.
● Don't store frozen bread dough in freezer for more than two months.
● If frozen bread dough thaws, do not refreeze before baking. If you do, bread will not rise properly.

BERRY CREAM SCONES

MAKES 8 TO 10

SCONES
2 cups biscuit baking mix
¼ cup sugar
¼ cup butter or margarine, melted
  and cooled
about ½ to ⅔ cup milk

FILLING
¾ cup heavy cream
1 to 2 tablespoons confectioners
  sugar
½ teaspoon vanilla
½ cup strawberry jam or preserves
  or favorite jam

1. Scones: Preheat oven to 425°F. Stir biscuit mix and sugar together in bowl. Stir in melted butter and enough milk to make a soft dough. Place dough on lightly floured surface and knead several strokes, or until smooth. Roll dough out to ½-inch thickness. Cut into rounds with floured 2½-inch biscuit cutter. Place rounds on ungreased cookie sheet, spacing them about 1 inch apart.

2. Brush tops of scones with milk. Bake 10 to 12 minutes, or until golden brown. Remove from cookie sheet and cool on wire racks.

3. Filling: Beat cream with confectioners sugar and vanilla until thick but not firm. Split scones in half while they are still warm. Spread bottom of each scone with 1 tablespoon jam. Top each with heaping dollop of whipped cream. Replace tops and serve.

VARIATION
Raisin Scones: Prepare dough as directed above, adding ¼ cup raisins or currants to biscuit mix mixture. Omit filling. Serve warm with sweet butter.

HINTS AND TIPS
Scones do not keep well in the refrigerator and are best when eaten the day they are made. However, they can be made ahead and frozen. Remove from oven and let cool completely. Place in a freezer storage bag, seal, label and freeze for up to 6 months. Thaw in the bag at room temperature 1 hour. Reheat in a 300°F oven 3 to 5 minutes.

SWEET BUNS

MAKES 15 OR 16 BUNS

BUNS

1-pound loaf frozen white bread
dough
2 tablespoons butter or margarine,
melted
½ cup firmly packed light brown
sugar
1 teaspoon cinnamon
½ cup raisins

GLAZE

2 cups confectioners sugar
2 tablespoons milk or light cream
½ teaspoon vanilla

1. Buns: Thaw dough according to package directions. Place in greased bowl and turn to coat entire surface. Cover and let rise in warm, draft-free place about 1 hour, or until doubled in bulk. Punch dough down.

2. Grease 2 cookie sheets or a 9 × 13-inch baking pan. Roll dough out to a 12 × 16-inch rectangle. Brush dough with melted butter. Combine brown sugar, cinnamon and raisins in small bowl and toss with fork until well combined. Sprinkle evenly over dough. Starting at long end, tightly roll up dough, jelly-roll style. Pinch seam to seal and turn over, seam side down. Cut dough into 16 slices with very sharp knife.

3. Arrange 8 slices on each prepared cookie sheet, spacing them about 2 inches apart. Press each slice gently with heel of hand. OR, cut dough into 15 equal-size slices. Arrange slices, cut side up, in prepared baking pan, spacing them evenly apart to allow room for expansion. Cover and let rise in warm, draft-free place about 30 to 45 minutes, or until doubled in bulk.

4. Preheat oven to 375°F. Bake buns 15 to 18 minutes on cookie sheets, or 20 to 25 minutes in baking pan. Remove from oven; remove buns from cookie sheets and cool on wire racks, or leave buns in pan and cool in pan on wire rack.

5. Glaze: Combine confectioners sugar, milk and vanilla, stirring until smooth. Drizzle or spread over buns while they are still warm. Let stand until glaze is set.

VARIATIONS

Orange-Currant Buns: Prepare and roll out dough as directed above. Combine 1 tablespoon grated orange peel, ½ cup firmly packed light brown sugar, 1 teaspoon cinnamon and ¾ cup currants. Sprinkle over dough. Proceed as directed above.

Cinnamon-Nut Buns: Prepare and roll out dough as directed above. Combine ½ cup granulated sugar, 2 teaspoons cinnamon and ⅓ cup finely chopped walnuts, pecans or almonds. Sprinkle over dough. Proceed as directed above.

Lemon-Coconut Buns: Prepare and roll out dough as directed above. Combine 1 tablespoon grated lemon peel, ⅓ cup granulated sugar, 2 tablespoons light brown sugar and ½ cup flaked coconut. Sprinkle over dough. Proceed as directed above. When making glaze omit vanilla and substitute 2 tablespoons lemon juice for milk. Sprinkle tops of buns with flaked coconut, if desired.

Pecan Sticky Buns: Prepare and roll out dough as directed above. Heat 2 tablespoons butter, 2 tablespoons light corn syrup and ½ cup firmly packed light brown sugar in saucepan until butter is melted and

brown sugar is dissolved. Spread mixture in bottom of greased 9 × 13-inch baking pan. Toss ½ cup chopped pecans with ¼ cup firmly packed light brown sugar and ½ teaspoon cinnamon. Sprinkle over dough. Roll up dough and cut into slices as directed above. Arrange slices over mixture in pan. Bake as directed above. Let cool in pan on wire rack 2 minutes, invert from pan onto serving plate.

CHERRY CLOVERLEAF BUNS

MAKES 16

BUNS
½ cup milk
¼ cup butter or margarine
3 tablespoons sugar
1 package (13¾ ounces) hot roll
  mix
1 egg, beaten
⅓ cup chopped candied cherries
16 candied cherries
melted butter

GLAZE
1 cup confectioners sugar, sifted
1 tablespoon plus 1 teaspoon milk
  or light cream

1. Buns: Remove package of yeast from roll mix; set aside. Heat milk, ¼ cup butter and sugar in heavy saucepan over low heat, stirring until butter is melted. Remove from heat and cool to lukewarm (about 105°F). Pour milk mixture into large bowl and stir in yeast until dissolved. Add egg, chopped cherries and remaining contents of roll mix package. Stir with wooden spoon until mixture is well blended and dough forms a ball and comes away from sides of bowl.

2. Place dough on well-floured surface and knead about 3 to 4 minutes, or until dough is no longer sticky. Place in greased bowl and turn to coat entire surface. Cover and let rise in warm, draft-free place about 45 minutes, or until doubled in bulk.

3. Punch dough down and divide in half. Divide each half into 24 pieces. Shape each piece into 1-inch ball, pinching and tucking ends under. Grease 2 cookie sheets. Group 3 balls of dough together and place on prepared cookie sheet. Make 15 more groups in same manner, spacing groups about 2 inches apart. Place cherry in center of each group of balls. Cover and let rise in warm, draft-free place 20 minutes.

4. Preheat oven to 425°F. Uncover buns and brush tops with melted butter. Bake 15 to 17 minutes, or until golden brown. Remove from cookie sheets to wire racks.

5. Glaze: Combine confectioners sugar and milk until smooth. Drizzle over buns while they are still warm. Let stand on racks until buns are cool and glaze is set.

ROSY SWIRLED POUND CAKE

SERVES 12 TO 14

CAKE
4 eggs
¼ cup sugar
1 package (18½ ounces) yellow cake and pudding mix
1 cup dairy sour cream
¼ cup vegetable oil
1 teaspoon imitation strawberry extract
3 to 4 drops red food coloring

GLAZE
1 cup confectioners sugar
about 1 to 2 tablespoons milk or light cream
½ teaspoon vanilla
crystallized sugar flowers (optional)

1. Cake: Preheat oven to 350°F. Grease 10-inch springform pan with fluted bottom, 10-inch tube pan or 12-cup Bundt pan. Beat eggs in large mixing bowl until thick and lemon-colored. Add sugar and beat until light and fluffy. Add cake mix, sour cream, oil and ¼ cup water and beat until well blended. Beat at medium speed 3 minutes.

2. Remove 1½ cups batter and pour into small bowl. Add strawberry extract and food coloring; beat until well blended. Pour plain batter into prepared pan. Spoon strawberry-flavored batter in 4 mounds on top of plain batter. Swirl through cake with small, flat spatula or knife to create marbled effect. Smooth top.

3. Bake 45 to 50 minutes, or until cake tester inserted 2 inches from outside edge of cake comes out clean. Cool in pan on wire rack 15 minutes. Invert from pan onto rack and carefully remove side and bottom of pan. Cool completely on rack.

4. Glaze: Combine confectioners sugar, milk and vanilla; stir until smooth, adding enough milk to make runny consistency. Place cake on serving plate and spoon glaze over top, letting it run down sides. Decorate with crystallized sugar flowers and let stand until glaze is set.

HINTS AND TIPS

To keep the cake plate clean, remember to place strips of waxed paper under the cake before spooning the glaze over. Make one strip long enough to protect the exposed part of the dish in the center of the cake.

SUNSHINE LEMON LOAF

SERVES 6 TO 8

1 package (16 or 17 ounces) pound cake mix
6 tablespoons butter or margarine, softened
⅔ cup sugar
1 tablespoon grated lemon peel
3 eggs, separated
juice of 1 lemon
3 tablespoons orange juice
1 package (7½ ounces) white frosting mix
fresh or crystallized lemon slices (optional)

1. Prepare pound cake mix according to package directions, dividing batter equally between 2 greased 8 × 4-inch loaf pans. Bake and cool according to package directions. Freeze 1 cake for later use. Wash and regrease 8 × 4-inch loaf pan. Line bottom and sides of pan with waxed paper and grease the paper. Place cake on its side and cut into 3 horizontal layers.

2. Cream butter, sugar and lemon peel together until light and fluffy. Beat in egg yolks, 1 at a time, beating well after each addition. Beat in lemon juice. Beat egg whites until stiff peaks form and fold into lemon mixture.

3. Place bottom layer of cake in prepared pan and sprinkle with 1 tablespoon orange juice. Spread with half the lemon mixture. Top with second cake layer, sprinkle with 1 tablespoon juice, and spread with remaining lemon mixture. Top with last cake layer and sprinkle with remaining orange juice. Lightly press down cake with fingertips. Cover with aluminum foil and refrigerate several hours or overnight.

4. To serve, prepare frosting mix according to package directions. Remove cake from refrigerator, uncover and invert onto serving plate. Carefully peel off waxed paper. Spread frosting over sides and top of cake, swirling it decoratively. Decorate top of cake with slices of fresh or crystallized lemon.

APRICOT-CINNAMON LOAF

SERVES 8 TO 10

1 package (13¾ ounces) hot roll
  mix
¾ cup hot water (105°F to 115°F)
1 egg, beaten
3 tablespoons apricot jam or
  favorite jam or preserves,
  warmed
¼ cup firmly packed light brown
  sugar
2 teaspoons cinnamon
milk

1. Remove package of yeast from roll mix; set aside. Pour hot water into large bowl. Sprinkle yeast over hot water and stir to dissolve. Stir in beaten egg and remaining contents of roll mix package with wooden spoon until mixture is well blended and dough forms a ball and comes away from sides of bowl. Cover with clean towel and let rise in warm, draft-free place about 45 minutes, or until doubled in bulk.

2. Grease 9 x 5-inch loaf pan. Stir dough down with wooden spoon. Place on a well-floured surface and knead for 3 to 4 minutes, or until dough is no longer sticky, kneading in additional flour, if necessary. Roll dough out to an 8 x 14-inch rectangle. Brush jam over dough to within ½ inch of edges. Combine sugar and cinnamon and sprinkle over jam. Starting at a short end, roll up dough, jelly-roll style. Firmly press ends together, tuck under, and pinch bottom seam to seal. Place roll, seam side down, in prepared pan. Cover and let rise in warm, draft-free place about 30 minutes, or until dough reaches rim of pan.

3. Preheat oven to 375°F. Brush top of bread with milk and bake 30 to 35 minutes, or until top is golden brown and bottom sounds hollow when tapped. Cool in pan on wire rack 10 minutes. Remove from pan and cool completely on rack. Wrap in plastic wrap and store overnight before slicing.

HINTS AND TIPS

If you slice this bread while it is still warm, or too fresh, the filling will run out and the bread will pull apart because the filling will be sticky. This bread is best when served the day after it is baked so the filling can firm up and the bread can be sliced easily. Be sure to press the edges of bread tightly together to prevent the filling from running out during baking.

INDEX

Make your home special

Since 1922, millions of men and women have turned to *Better Homes and Gardens* magazine for help in making their homes more enjoyable places to be. You, too, can trust *Better Homes and Gardens* to provide you with the best in ideas, inspiration and information for better family living.

In every issue you'll find ideas on food and recipes, decorating and furnishings, crafts and hobbies, remodeling and building, gardening and outdoor living plus family money management, health, education, pets, car maintenance and more.

For information on how you can have *Better Homes and Gardens* delivered to your door, write to: Mr. Robert Austin, P.O. Box 4536, Des Moines, IA 50336.

Better Homes ®
and Gardens

*The Idea Magazine
for Better Homes
and Families*